JOHN MORTON

John Morton created, wrote and directed the television series *Twenty Twelve*, which won a BAFTA for Best Sitcom, and *W1A* which ran for three series. His latest series as creator, writer, director and executive producer, *Twenty Twenty Six*, premiered on BBC Two earlier this year.

His first comedy *People Like Us* began life on Radio 4 and transferred to BBC Two, winning the Royal Television Society Award for Best Comedy and the Silver Rose for Comedy at the Montreux Television Festival, as well as being nominated for a BAFTA, a British Comedy Award and a South Bank Show Award.

He was the writer, director and executive producer for *Ten Percent* (the UK version of *Call My Agent!*). Other television series: as writer, director and creator, *Broken News* and *The Gist*; as co-writer, *Kiss Me Kate*; as director, *Absolute Power*.

His radio series includes *Mightier Than the Sword* and *The Sunday Format*.

Eclipse is his first stage play.

John Morton

ECLIPSE

NICK HERN BOOKS

London

www.nickhernbooks.co.uk

A Nick Hern Book

Eclipse first published in Great Britain in 2026 as a paperback original by Nick Hern Books Limited, The Glasshouse, 49a Goldhawk Road, London W12 8QP

Eclipse copyright © 2026 John Morton

John Morton has asserted his moral right to be identified as the author of this work

Cover image by Bob King Creative for Chichester Festival Theatre, photo by Seamus Ryan.

Designed and typeset by Nick Hern Books, London
Printed in the UK by Mimeo Ltd, Huntingdon, Cambridgeshire PE29 6XX

A CIP catalogue record for this book is available from the British Library

ISBN 978 1 83904 578 3

CAUTION   All rights whatsoever in this play are strictly reserved. Requests to reproduce the text in whole or in part should be addressed to the publisher. This book may not be used, in whole or in part, for the development or training of artificial intelligence technologies or systems.

Amateur Performing Rights   Applications for performance, including readings and excerpts, by amateurs in the English language throughout the world should be addressed to the Performing Rights Department, Nick Hern Books, The Glasshouse, 49a Goldhawk Road, London W12 8QP, *tel* +44 (0)20 8749 4953, *email* rights@nickhernbooks.co.uk, except as follows:

Australia: ORiGiN Theatrical, Level 1, 213 Clarence Street, Sydney NSW 2000, *tel* +61 (2) 8514 5201, *email* enquiries@originmusic.com.au, *web* www.origintheatrical.com.au

New Zealand: Play Bureau, 20 Rua Street, Mangapapa, Gisborne, 4010, *tel* +64 21 258 3998, *email* info@playbureau.com

United States and Canada: Curtis Brown Ltd, see details below

Professional Performing Rights   Applications for performance by professionals in any medium and in any language throughout the world should be addressed to Curtis Brown Ltd, Cunard House, 15 Regent Street, St James's, London SW1Y 4LR, *tel* +44 (0)20 7393 4400, *fax* +44 (0)20 7393 4401, *email* cb@curtisbrown.co.uk

No performance of any kind may be given unless a licence has been obtained. Applications should be made before rehearsals begin. Publication of this play does not necessarily indicate its availability for amateur performance.

www.nickhernbooks.co.uk/environmental-policy

Nick Hern Books' authorised representative in the EU is
Easy Access System Europe – Mustamäe tee 50, 10621 Tallinn, Estonia
email gpsr.requests@easproject.com

Eclipse was produced by Chichester Festival Theatre and first performed in the Minerva Theatre, Chichester, on 8 May 2026 with the following cast (in order of speaking):

KAREN	Selina Cadell
POSTMAN	Brendan Hooper
SARAH	Sarah Parish
JONATHAN	Rupert Penry-Jones
GRAHAM	Paul Thornley
LINDA	Lizzie Hopley
MILKMAN	Julian Protheroe
NELL	Mariam Haque
JULIA	Katharine Bennett-Fox
DR PARKER	Maanuv Thiara

Director	John Morton
Designer	Simon Higlett
Lighting Designer	Emma Chapman
Sound Design and Music	Ed Clarke
Movement Director	Mike Ashcroft
Casting Director	Matilda James CDG
Associate Director	Fiona Dunn
Voice & Dialect Coach	Tess Dignan
Production Manager	John Page
Costume Supervisor	Rachael Griffin
Props Supervisor	Tegan Cutts
Company Stage Manager	David Curl
Deputy Stage Manager	Sophie Macfadyen
Assistant Stage Manager	Jenny Wood

Eclipse was originally commissioned and developed by ROYO, in association with Wessex Grove.

Characters

JONATHAN, *late forties. The son that moved away*
SARAH, *mid-forties. Jonathan's sister. The daughter that stayed*
GRAHAM, *mid-forties. Sarah's husband*
NELL, *mid-forties. Ex-partner of Jonathan*
KAREN, *sixties. Local authority care assistant. Devon*
LINDA, *fifties. CareWatch Team Supervisor. Lancashire*
JULIA, *thirties. NHS nurse*
DR PARKER, *forties. GP*
POSTMAN, *fifties. Devon*
MILKMAN, *sixties. Devon*

The action takes pace over the course of twenty-four hours in late summer.

Setting

The kitchen of an old house, once a rectory, in Devon. Late summer.

Windows look out onto trees, a big old garden. The sense of hills beyond.

The kitchen, the house generally, hasn't been updated for at least a generation.

Prominent amongst the jumble of things on a sideboard is an old cuddly toy-style badger.

Above it on the wall is a handsome painting of the house, painted from under an old tree.

Upstage, a lobby off the kitchen leading to the door of The Room, into which people come and go. We never see what's inside it.

Downstage, a door to the outside – the back door to the house (open) – leading to an area which represents the beginning of an old garden. A sense of mature overhanging trees, an old magnolia, lush vegetation beyond.

This is a place where time has stood still.

This text went to press before the end of rehearsals and so may differ slightly from the play as performed.

ACT ONE

Scene One, Morning

Music – the play's simple spare theme – establishes itself and slowly fades.

From somewhere not too far away a church clock strikes ten as a POSTMAN *arrives along the path in the morning sunshine to the (open) back door. Thinks about knocking, decides not to. Instead, he leaves some mail on the back step.*

He turns to go. On the way back he meets KAREN *coming along the path carrying a bag.*

KAREN. Morning.

POSTMAN. Morning. 'Nother nice one.

KAREN. Beautiful idn't it? Perfect.

POSTMAN. Is it ever going to end?

KAREN. Shan't complain if it don't.

POSTMAN. I left the post on the step there.

KAREN. Oh right.

POSTMAN. I didn't like to knock.

KAREN. I'll take them in with me that's fine.

POSTMAN. Okay. See you then.

KAREN. See you.

POSTMAN. Yep.

KAREN. Bye.

The POSTMAN *continues back up the path and off.*

KAREN *continues to the back door, picks up the mail from the step, knocks cursorily on the open door and continues straight in.*

(*Shouting ahead.*) Morning.

No response.

Hello?

Unperturbed, she puts the bag and the mail down on the table and crosses to flick the kettle on after feeling it for warmth first. All routine.

As the turns she notices something she hasn't seen before – the badger on the sideboard across the room.

She crosses to look at it more closely. Stands it front of it, leans down to its level, looks it in the eye. A moment where she's trying to decide whether to pick it up or not, as if worried that someone might see her.

Just as she's decided to pick it up, SARAH *arrives through the lobby leading from The Room and she puts it straight back down again.*

SARAH. Hi.

KAREN. Oh hi Sarah. Morning.

SARAH (*confirming*). I thought I heard a voice out here.

KAREN. Yes. How are you today.

SARAH. Oh you know, yes.

KAREN. Beautiful morning isn't it?

SARAH. Yes.

KAREN. I brought the mail in.

SARAH. Oh great, thanks.

SARAH *has a cursory look at the envelopes. Doesn't open any of them.*

KAREN. No, perfect it is. That scent you get when you come down the path –

SARAH. Oh the magnolia –

KAREN. – Magnolia –

SARAH. – yes.

KAREN. – Magnolia yeah I thought it was yeah. Yeah lovely this morning it is when you come in the gate. I come the other way this morning, you know round by Topsham Bridge?

SARAH. Oh right.

As she continues, KAREN *takes her cardigan off, gets out a blue nursing-style smock from her bag, and slips it on, adjusts it. A daily routine.*

KAREN. Yeah my Roger, he was on at me to keep on the main road, case I meet anything like. I don't think he trusts me with his new car.

SARAH. Oh okay yes I saw that at the gate yesterday then.

KAREN. Yeah –

SARAH. Nice.

KAREN. – he's always wanted a Honda. I don't know why.

SARAH. No.

KAREN. I said I'd stay on the main road, I promised like. But I went round Topsham Bridge anyway.

SARAH. Right.

KAREN. Beautiful it was. Really beautiful.

The kettle boils and switches off.

I've put the kettle on.

SARAH. Yes.

KAREN. You're probably ready for a cup of tea –

SARAH. Oh no thanks Karen –

KAREN. – or a coffee or something.

SARAH. – no.

KAREN. You sure?

SARAH. I was thinking I might nip home and have a shower –

KAREN. Yes –

SARAH. – you know if you're okay with –

KAREN. – of course. No you go Sarah, you go.

Crossing to a yellow plastic file on the table, flicking through to the most recent entry.

How is he this morning?

SARAH. Uhh well, I mean you know –

KAREN. Yes.

SARAH. – not great.

KAREN. No. Has he had any breakfast?

SARAH. No, not really.

KAREN. No.

SARAH. He had a bit of juice.

KAREN. Yes.

(*Squinting at the file.*) Honestly my eyes –

SARAH. Oh I know –

KAREN. I can't read a thing.

SARAH. – I know how you feel.

KAREN. Happens to us all eventually.

SARAH. Yes.

KAREN (*getting a pair of reading glasses from her bag*). You should get some of these.

SARAH. Right.

KAREN. They're brilliant they are. Twelve pound fifty from Boots.

SARAH. Really?

KAREN. They got hundreds in there they have, different styles and that.

SARAH. Well that's –

KAREN (*handing them to her to try*). Here.

SARAH. Thanks.

KAREN. I've had it with opticians – varifocals, special coatings and that.

SARAH. Yes.

KAREN. Twelve pounds fifty. Put them on.

SARAH (*trying them on*). Yes. Yes no they're really –

KAREN. That's all you need really. Everything nice and big.

SARAH (*handing them back*). Yes, thanks great.

KAREN (*from the file*). He still hasn't had his Oramorph then.

SARAH. No. Still won't take it.

KAREN. No. I'll go in and say hello –

SARAH. Yes –

KAREN. – have a bit of a natter.

SARAH. – yes well good luck with that.

KAREN. Jonathan's not back yet then.

SARAH. Jonathan.

KAREN. Yes.

SARAH. No.

KAREN. No. I know Edward was asking where he was yesterday.

SARAH. Yes. No he was supposed to, he was going to get the last train back, but he texted to say he didn't make it.

KAREN. Right. Well I'll go in and see what's what.

SARAH. Okay well, you sure you're okay for a bit.

KAREN. Course I am.

SARAH. You've got my number if –

KAREN. You go, get yourself sorted. Take your time. That's what I'm here for.

SARAH. Okay well thanks. Thanks.

KAREN *crosses to the lobby leading to The Room (off) and opens the door.*

KAREN (*brightly*). Hello Edward.

(*Going in.*) How are you today? It's a beautiful morning…

The door closes gently behind her. Pause.

In the kitchen, SARAH *picks up her bag and stands motionless in the middle of the room, taking in the silence and stillness. Birdsong from outside. It's as if she's stalled.*

Then she becomes aware of another sound.

Outside, a voice approaching talking on the phone.
JONATHAN *arrives slowly along the path with a crumpled*
overnight shoulder bag.

JONATHAN (*on phone*). But I mean wow that's fantastic…
Well isn't it?… What did I say I *told* you, I had a feeling…
What d'you mean. Why?… Of *course* it is. I wish I could
have stayed, we could have I don't know we could have gone
out for a slap-up breakfast or you know… But you're going
to take it, right? You're gonna take it? Cos… Sorry what?…
Okay no Em you're breaking up again. Em?

Pacing to try to find a signal.

Em you're breaking up I can't – Em? No this is, I've lost you
I'll call you back okay. Congratulations, I'll call you. Em?

The signal's gone.

Right.

He hangs up.

Pause.

He stands looking down at the phone in his hand.

Then he looks up, taking in the garden around him, the
birdsong, the house, before continuing to the back door and
into the kitchen.

SARAH. Hi.

JONATHAN. Oh hi.

SARAH. You're back.

JONATHAN. Yes –

SARAH (*glancing at her watch*). I didn't expect to see you this
early.

JONATHAN. – no well I caught the early train.

SARAH. Right.

JONATHAN (*putting his bag down*). Hang on what the hell's
this doing here?

JONATHAN *crosses to the badger.*

SARAH. I found him upstairs at the back of the airing cupboard.

JONATHAN (*picking it up*). God.

SARAH. I thought I'd bring him out.

JONATHAN. Amazing. I had no idea.

SARAH. It didn't seem fair he should be in there somehow.

JONATHAN. Fair.

SARAH. Yes. With all the old linen.

JONATHAN. Dad would have a fit if he knew.

SARAH. Yes. Still, he's not going to be coming in here any more is he. So.

JONATHAN. He's in pretty good shape for someone who's been in an airing cupboard for twenty years.

SARAH. That's what I thought.

JONATHAN (*putting the badger back down*). I'm going to put the kettle on I've just realised I'm starving.

Crossing to flick the kettle on.

SARAH. It should still be warm. Didn't you get any breakfast?

JONATHAN. Breakfast?

SARAH. Yes.

JONATHAN. What *on the train*?

SARAH. Oh right. Okay.

JONATHAN. That's a joke right?

SARAH. Well it's no wonder then.

JONATHAN. What about you.

SARAH. Me?

JONATHAN. Have you had anything?

SARAH. No –

JONATHAN. So –

SARAH. – I'm not really hungry –

JONATHAN. *Really?*

SARAH. – not really.

JONATHAN. Well I'm gonna make some toast.

SARAH. I might have something later.

JONATHAN. Okay.

> As they continue, JONATHAN *crosses to assemble bread board, bread knife, and loaf of bread.*

> So how's it been?

SARAH. How's it been?

JONATHAN. What sort of a night was it?

SARAH. Uhh well – Karen's here now –

JONATHAN. Yes I saw the car.

SARAH. – it was okay. I was up four times.

JONATHAN. No.

SARAH. Yes.

JONATHAN. Four?

SARAH (*indicating a chair*). I ended up coming down and sleeping down here –

JONATHAN. What down here?

SARAH. Yes.

JONATHAN. God.

SARAH. I know, I think I've done something to my neck. I was so scared of falling asleep and not hearing that bloody whistle.

JONATHAN. I did try to get back you know.

SARAH (*if you say so*). Yes I'm sure.

JONATHAN. But it just, things got a bit –

SARAH (*as above*). Yes.

JONATHAN (*sawing at the loaf with the knife*). God, honestly –

SARAH. What.

JONATHAN. – fucking bread knife.

SARAH (*agreement*). Oh no –

JONATHAN. I mean it's just –

SARAH. – no it's useless, it doesn't work.

JONATHAN (*sawing*). – Christ's sake –

The loaf starts to disintegrate under the blunt knife.

SARAH. It was one of Mum's famous bargains from that stall at Kingsbridge show every year.

JONATHAN. It's like everything –

SARAH. She bought a whole set of them – they were all useless.

JONATHAN. – I mean how the hell has he managed?

SARAH. He bought sliced bread.

JONATHAN. Yes.

(*Trying to stuff two mangled slices of bread into the toaster.*) And if you do manage to hack something off you have to do battle with the fucking toaster.

SARAH. Yes.

JONATHAN. That's a whole other thing.

As they continue, JONATHAN keeps pushing the lever on the toaster down. It keeps springing straight back up again. He tries altering the settings, manually holding the lever down. It still won't stay down.

SARAH. Oh also, he's still not taking the morphine stuff.

JONATHAN. No. Course not.

SARAH. I tried. He just pushed it away.

JONATHAN (*ramming the toaster down repeatedly*). Yes.

SARAH. Wouldn't take any sleeping pills either.

JONATHAN. Right.

(*The toaster – a decision.*) Right. Okay.

He switches the toaster off at the wall, unplugs it, plugs it straight back again, switches it back on and tries again. This time it stays down.

Good.

The kettle has boiled and flicks off.

Coffee?

SARAH. I was thinking about nipping back home for a shower –

JONATHAN. Okay.

SARAH. – but if you're having something I might as well –

JONATHAN. Yes.

SARAH. – I'll have a cup of tea.

JONATHAN. Tea, okay. Right.

The toast in the toaster pings up noisily. JONATHAN *rams it straight back down again.*

SARAH. So how was it?

JONATHAN. How was what.

SARAH. London.

JONATHAN. Oh, right. No I mean it was just a couple of meetings –

SARAH. Yes.

JONATHAN. – you know. I picked up some mail.

SARAH. Right.

Beat. The toast pings up again. JONATHAN *rams it straight back down again.*

You saw Emma.

JONATHAN. Emma?

SARAH. Yeah.

JONATHAN. What? Yes no I saw her last night yes.

SARAH. So is she going to come down?

JONATHAN. Uh yes I mean it's tricky at the moment.

SARAH. Right.

JONATHAN. It's all a bit – She's actually just got offered this job.

SARAH. Oh right.

JONATHAN. Yes –

SARAH. An acting job.

JONATHAN. – yeah quite a big Netflix thing.

SARAH. Oh right. Where?

JONATHAN. Where?

SARAH. Yes.

JONATHAN. Well, I mean it's Los Angeles actually.

SARAH. Los Angeles?

JONATHAN. Yes.

SARAH. Right.

JONATHAN. Yes. So you know, so it's a quite a big thing.

SARAH. Yes.

The toast pings up again. JONATHAN *rams it back down again.*

And what about Nell?

JONATHAN. Nell?

SARAH. Yes.

JONATHAN. Right, yes –

SARAH. You said you were going to phone her.

JONATHAN. – no no –

SARAH. Yeah, so –

JONATHAN. – no I spoke to her.

SARAH. You've spoken to her.

JONATHAN. Yes.

SARAH. Right. Okay.

JONATHAN. I phoned her.

Beat.

SARAH. How is she.

JONATHAN. How *is* she?

SARAH. Yes.

JONATHAN. I mean she's okay I think.

SARAH. You *think.*

JONATHAN. I mean –

SARAH. Well what did you actually say to her.

JONATHAN. Well –

SARAH. You *told* her.

JONATHAN. Well yes.

SARAH. So is she going to come down?

JONATHAN. Look she wasn't *there* okay.

SARAH. She wasn't *there.*

JONATHAN. I left a message.

SARAH (*typical*). Oh right okay.

Beat.

D'you want her to come?

JONATHAN. I mean it's difficult –

SARAH. Yes –

JONATHAN. – you know, it's –

SARAH. – yes no I'm sure it is. It must be.

Beat.

JONATHAN. Look I know what you –

SARAH. That doesn't matter.

JONATHAN. No I'm just –

SARAH. It doesn't matter what I think, that's irrelevant.
Everyone must do what they think is right.

JONATHAN. Yes.

In the lobby, the door to The Room opens. KAREN *comes out and crosses into the kitchen.*

KAREN. Hi.

JONATHAN. Hi Karen.

KAREN. Oh hi Jonathan. You're back.

JONATHAN. Yes I'm back yes.

KAREN. Sorry to bother you straight away but you haven't got a minute have you?

JONATHAN. Yes. Me?

KAREN. I mean only if –

JONATHAN. Yes no of course yes.

KAREN. – it's just I think we should probably change him again.

JONATHAN. Right.

SARAH. Okay. Again? –

KAREN. I mean I suppose we *could* wait for Linda to arrive –

SARAH. – no it's okay. I'll do it.

JONATHAN. No no –

SARAH. You stay and have your toast.

KAREN. It's just someone to work the hoist really.

JONATHAN. Yes.

SARAH. Well I can do that.

JONATHAN. No it's okay –

SARAH. I did it yesterday.

JONATHAN. – I mean you're going back to have a shower aren't you?

SARAH. That's okay I can have a shower later.

JONATHAN. Right.

KAREN. To be fair Sarah, Edward is asking for Jonathan.

SARAH. Oh right.

JONATHAN. Right.

KAREN. Least I think that's what he's saying anyway.

SARAH. Fine.

   KAREN *sniffing*.

JONATHAN. What.

KAREN. Is that –

JONATHAN (*diving for the toaster*). Shit, the toast!

KAREN. Oh dear.

JONATHAN. Fuck!

   Smoke is coming out of the toaster. JONATHAN scrabbles to force the toast up. More smoke and two black slices.

KAREN (*definitive assessment*). Oh no –

JONATHAN. Brilliant.

   JONATHAN *manages to juggle the charred slices over to the pedal bin and drop them in.*

KAREN. – that's no good.

JONATHAN. Ow! Fucking brilliant.

SARAH. It's alright you go in.

JONATHAN. No but, really?

SARAH. I'll put some more on. I suppose if it's a choice between the toaster and the hoist – I mean that is a tough one.

JONATHAN. Okay well –

SARAH. I'll bring it in. And coffee.

JONATHAN. – great, thanks. Good luck.

SARAH. Yes you too.

   JONATHAN *crosses with* KAREN *back to the lobby.*
   KAREN *pushes the door to The Room open.*

KAREN (*as she goes in*). Right. Look who I've got here Edward –

JONATHAN (*as he goes in*). Hi Dad.

KAREN. – I got Jonathan here.

JONATHAN. How are things.

KAREN. Jonathan's back.

JONATHAN. It's a fabulous morning out there.

The door swings gently closed behind them. Beat.

In the kitchen, SARAH crosses to confront the deformed loaf of bread, picks up the blunt knife, but then seems to stall again.

She can't face it.

She stands there, head bowed, breathing.

Scene Two, Morning

In the garden outside the back door.

SARAH with a washing basket trying to hang out some big sheets and pyjamas in the sunshine on a washing carousel. It's not easy on her own.

JONATHAN appears around the corner from the garden with a coffee mug, now empty.

JONATHAN. Hi.

SARAH. Hi.

JONATHAN. D'you want a hand.

SARAH. No I'm fine thanks.

JONATHAN (*taking one end of a sheet*). Here –

SARAH. Careful with that.

JONATHAN. I am being.

SARAH. No it's –

JONATHAN. Yes alright –

SARAH. – on the dirty ground.

JONATHAN. – yes I know okay. Look, why don't we just –

SARAH (*I can do this*). – Yes okay –

JONATHAN. – then we can –

SARAH. Yes. Okay. Thanks.

JONATHAN. Okay?

SARAH. Okay thanks.

They peg the sheet out together.

JONATHAN. How is it in there.

SARAH. He's quieter now, he's got his eyes closed.

JONATHAN. Right.

SARAH. He's tired.

JONATHAN. Yes. God. Poor Dad.

They finish pegging the sheet out.

I wonder what Mum would have made of all this.

SARAH. God yes.

JONATHAN. She'd have –

SARAH. Well she'd have been –

JONATHAN. Yes –

SARAH. – it's just as well things happened this way round.

JONATHAN. Yes.

Pause.

Okay well –

SARAH. So by the way I spoke to Nell.

JONATHAN. You spoke to her?

SARAH. Yes. She phoned me.

JONATHAN. *She* phoned *you*.

SARAH. Yes.

JONATHAN. When.

SARAH. When?

JONATHAN. Yes, when was this?

SARAH. What d'you mean when.

JONATHAN. When did she phone you.

SARAH. She wanted to know whether I thought she should come down.

JONATHAN (*clarification*). Whether *you* thought –

SARAH. If I thought it would be awkward.

JONATHAN. Oh okay.

SARAH. Yes.

JONATHAN. Right.

Beat.

So what did you say.

SARAH. Well what d'you expect me to say. I said if she wanted to come, if she wanted to see Dad, that's the only thing that matters.

JONATHAN. Yes.

SARAH. But I said if she was thinking about it, you know just come, don't hang around that's all.

JONATHAN. Right well that's, yes.

Pause.

Then GRAHAM arrives along the path wearing shorts and sturdy boots.

GRAHAM. Hi.

SARAH. Oh –

JONATHAN. Hi Graham.

GRAHAM. Hi Jonathan.

SARAH. – what are *you* doing here?

GRAHAM. I thought I might just look in on my way past –

SARAH. I *thought* I heard a car.

GRAHAM. – maybe do a bit of mowing or something.

JONATHAN. Right.

SARAH. *Mowing?*

GRAHAM. Maybe, yes. I don't know.

SARAH. I thought you were *working* this morning.

GRAHAM. Yeah I am yeah, I was.

SARAH. You could have fooled me.

GRAHAM. No I went over to Crannacombe but the guy wasn't there.

SARAH. He wasn't there.

GRAHAM. No.

SARAH. What d'you mean he wasn't there.

GRAHAM. I don't know, I got a message from the office.
So I did what I could, took some measurements and photos:
I thought I might look in here on my way back past.

JONATHAN. Yes well it's good to see you.

GRAHAM. Beautiful day isn't it?

JONATHAN. Isn't it fabulous.

GRAHAM. It's perfect. How *is* Edward this morning?

SARAH. How *is* he?

GRAHAM. Yes.

JONATHAN. Well he's really weak now.

GRAHAM. Yes. Mind you we've been saying that for weeks.

JONATHAN. I know but really, he's not really drinking anything –

GRAHAM. No.

JONATHAN. – he's not eating anything.

GRAHAM. Yes.

JONATHAN. He's got a different look about him now.

GRAHAM. Right.

Beat.

Oh well, best get on I suppose.

JONATHAN. You don't want a quick cup of tea before you –

GRAHAM. No thanks Jonathan, thank you. I thought I might do a bit round the orchard.

JONATHAN. Right, yes.

SARAH. The orchard.

GRAHAM. Yes.

SARAH. I thought you did that yesterday.

GRAHAM. Or maybe up at the top there up behind the rhododendrons.

JONATHAN. Well great if you've got the time.

SARAH. Anyway you're too early I'm afraid.

GRAHAM. What?

SARAH. She's not here yet.

JONATHAN. Who isn't here?

SARAH. Julia the nurse.

JONATHAN. What?

GRAHAM. Look I thought I'd come over, I thought I'd do some mowing okay?

SARAH. Yes, and with a bit of luck if you stretch it out long enough you might just get lucky.

GRAHAM (*turning to go*). Right. Okay. I don't care –

SARAH. Graham.

GRAHAM. – I won't bother I won't do it, mow your own bloody grass.

SARAH. Don't be silly I was –

GRAHAM (*turning back*). It's two-and-a-half acres out here.

SARAH. – yes –

GRAHAM. The number of hours I've spent out here –

SARAH. I know.

GRAHAM. – I mean before, even when your mum was alive.

SARAH. Yes.

JONATHAN. Yes.

GRAHAM. Someone's got to look after it. Otherwise what's going to happen to it all? Someone's got to look after it all.

GRAHAM *strides off around the path to the garden and off.*

SARAH. He'll be alright, he'll cool down –

JONATHAN. He has done a lot in the last few years.

SARAH. I know he has.

JONATHAN. He's really taken it on.

SARAH. I know. It's only cos it's true. I can read him like a book.

Pause.

JONATHAN. I was thinking when I was walking round, I don't think I've ever seen it look so beautiful.

SARAH. No.

JONATHAN. God knows how Dad ever did it all on his own. And the magnolia this year –

SARAH. Yes –

JONATHAN. – I mean it's just, it's –

SARAH (*the family story*). – yes well of course that is why he came here.

JONATHAN. Yes.

SARAH. Why we came here: when he came down the path, round the corner, and caught the scent.

JONATHAN. Yes.

SARAH. Don't know whether that's true or not.

JONATHAN. No.

SARAH. Might just be another one of his, you know –

JONATHAN. Yes. I don't know though. On a morning like this.

Beat.

One of my first memories, first memory of anything really, I don't know how old I was, must have been really small: it was still light outside – I was in the small room at the front – the sound of Dad mowing somewhere down under the plane tree outside as I went to sleep, the smell of cut grass. Must have been summer.

Long pause. They stand there.

Birdsong.

I can't believe I won't be able to come here. I can't believe it.

From somewhere in the garden, the sound of a lawn mower starting up.

Scene Three, Morning

In the kitchen, GRAHAM has the toaster unplugged, unscrewed, and upside down over some newspaper near the sink and is prodding away at its innards with a screwdriver.

GRAHAM (*to himself*). Cuh… Cuh…

Outside, a woman arrives along the path: LINDA, Lancashire accent, thick glasses, wearing what looks like a cross between a nurse's uniform and supermarket checkout livery and carrying a bag.

LINDA (*at the door*). Hiya.

GRAHAM. Hello?

LINDA (*coming straight in*). Can I come in?

GRAHAM. Oh hi Linda. How are you.

LINDA. Another cracking one.

GRAHAM. Lovely isn't it.

LINDA. What I did, I came off the main road at Halwell this morning on my way over and cut down through Moreleigh is it?

GRAHAM. Oh yes, Moreleigh yes.

LINDA. Oh it's lovely it was.

GRAHAM. Yes.

LINDA. Fabulous. Now is it just me or can I smell burning in here?

GRAHAM. Yes you can yes.

LINDA. I thought so.

GRAHAM. Yeah –

LINDA. As soon as I caught wind of it, I thought to myself I thought hey up that'll be the toaster up to its tricks again.

GRAHAM. – yeah no what it is, no one's bothered to clean it out for years, that's what it is.

LINDA. Yes –

GRAHAM (*prodding*). *Look* at it here. Virtually solid.

LINDA. – no I like a good explanation, me.

LINDA *puts her bag down, crosses to the yellow file on the table and flicks through the most recent pages.*

Right. How are things this morning.

GRAHAM. Oh well you know, not so bad I don't think. I mean not great obviously.

LINDA. No.

GRAHAM. They're all in there with him now.

LINDA. Has Julia been yet.

GRAHAM. No she hasn't. Who?

LINDA. Julia, the nurse.

GRAHAM. Yeah. No she hasn't been yet I don't think.

LINDA (*finished with the file*). No. Right. I'll go in and see what's what.

(*Noticing the badger on the sideboard*.) Ooh hello who's this?

GRAHAM. Oh yeah –

LINDA (*crossing to it*). What is it a mongoose?

GRAHAM. A *mongoose*?

LINDA. I don't mean mongoose do I.

GRAHAM. Yeah no that's Brian.

LINDA. Brian?

GRAHAM. Brian the badger yeah.

LINDA (*picking it up*). Of course yes, *badger* yes –

GRAHAM. Sarah found him in a cupboard or something.

LINDA (*to Brian*). – you're a *badger* aren't you of course you are, hello Brian. Honestly what am I like. You're a nice little chap aren't you?

In the lobby, the door to The Room opens.

KAREN *comes out wearing latex gloves and carrying a scrunched-up ball of bed sheets and pyjamas, a plastic bucket and a plastic shopping bag (full) tied tightly at the top, followed by* JONATHAN.

KAREN (*back through the door*). – we'll be back in a minute Edward. See about that yogurt.

JONATHAN (*back through the door*). Back in a minute Dad. You okay for a minute Sarah?

SARAH (*off*). Yes I'll stay here. Okay Dad?

The door swings closed as they cross to the kitchen.

KAREN. Morning.

LINDA. Hiya.

JONATHAN. Hi Linda.

LINDA *is still holding Brian.*

KAREN. I see you made a friend there.

LINDA. Yes this is Brian yes –

KAREN. Brian?

JONATHAN. Yes –

LINDA. Brian the badger.

KAREN. I *wondered* who he was.

JONATHAN. It's not the original one, we lost that. That was one the publishers sent when they sold the film rights.

LINDA. The *film* rights.

JONATHAN. Dad always hated it.

GRAHAM. Sarah found him in a cupboard.

KAREN. He hated it?

JONATHAN. He wouldn't have it around.

GRAHAM. You know all the *Brian the Badger* books that Edward wrote.

LINDA. The what, love?

GRAHAM. Oh, right.

LINDA. Sorry –

GRAHAM. Yeah he wrote all these books?

LINDA. – right –

GRAHAM. Yeah loads of them.

LINDA. – no I don't know what it is but I'm not a great reader, me.

GRAHAM. He was actually quite famous at one time wasn't he Jonathan.

JONATHAN. I don't know about famous.

GRAHAM. He was. He was interviewed by Angela Rippon.

JONATHAN. Yes, well. Anyway.

LINDA (*putting Brian down*). So how's things?

KAREN. Yes –

LINDA. How is Edward this morning.

KAREN. – we've had a bit of a busy morning so far –

JONATHAN. Yes.

KAREN. Sarah's in there with him at the moment. We just finished changing him again.

LINDA. Oh right.

KAREN. He wasn't very keen on it was he Jonathan.

JONATHAN. Not really no.

LINDA. No I bet.

KAREN. Poor Edward. He's been up and down on that hoist like a yo-yo.

LINDA. Yes.

KAREN. But he's more comfortable now. We give him a bit of clean-round like, best we could –

LINDA. Brilliant.

KAREN. – yeah so you timed it just right this morning.

LINDA. I'll give him a moment to settle down then I'll go in and see what's what.

KAREN. Yes.

As they continue, KAREN *stuffs the bed sheets into the washing machine, puts powder in and turns it on.*

LINDA. I was just saying to Graham, what I did this morning, I came off the main road and came down through Moreleigh.

KAREN. Oh yes Moreleigh, yes.

LINDA. Yes. It's a much better route for me.

KAREN. Yes.

LINDA. Mind you I say that, it depends where I'm coming from.

KAREN. What I done today, I came over through Loddiswell and then up through Topsham Bridge?

LINDA. Oh right yes.

KAREN. Yes.

LINDA. I've never heard of that.

KAREN. Lovely it was, really beautiful.

(*The tightly tied shopping bag.*) I don't know what you want to do with this Jonathan.

JONATHAN. Right uh –

(*Taking it.*) – thanks. Think I'll put it outside in the bin.

KAREN. Really speaking, you should have proper orange bags for that.

LINDA. Yes.

JONATHAN. Yes I know.

GRAHAM. Yeah.

KAREN. The bin men, they're within their rights to refuse to take clinical waste products.

JONATHAN. Yes –

LINDA. Oh yes they can refuse to take it. It's within their rights.

GRAHAM. Yeah, it is.

JONATHAN. – I know, I phoned the council but I didn't get anywhere. I must have another try.

GRAHAM. I'll put the kettle on shall I.

JONATHAN. Yes good idea.

GRAHAM (*filling up the kettle*). Sarah says Nell might be coming down.

JONATHAN. Well uh –

GRAHAM. That'd be nice wouldn't it.

JONATHAN. – yes I mean –

GRAHAM. After all this time.

JONATHAN. – yes. So what are you actually –

GRAHAM. I was just having a go at the toaster here.

JONATHAN. Yes so I see.

GRAHAM. It's no wonder, you should have seen it it's virtually solid here.

JONATHAN. Right.

GRAHAM. All it is, it's just the release mechanism, no one's thought to clean it out, that's all it is.

JONATHAN. Yes.

(*The shopping bag.*) In the meantime I am going to put this outside in the bin, whether they arrest me or not.

GRAHAM. Right.

GRAHAM *crosses to flick the kettle on.*

JONATHAN *crosses to the back door. Outside there's a dustbin against a wall. He lifts the lid, drops the bag in.*

LINDA (*confirming*). He hasn't had any breakfast then.

KAREN. He doesn't want any no –

LINDA. Right.

KAREN (*crossing to the fridge*). – but he says he might have a bit of yogurt.

LINDA. Oh right yes, yogurt.

KAREN (*opening the fridge door*). Maybe we can get him to take his Oramorph at the same time.

LINDA. Yes, I like your thinking.

KAREN (*taking out individual yogurt pots and peering at them one at a time*). I can't remember what flavour it is Edward likes. Strawberry is it? Or was it black cherry? I don't think it was rhubarb.

LINDA. I think he had a vanilla one the other morning.

KAREN. Vanilla?

LINDA. I think so yes.

KAREN. Right.

LINDA. I think he quite liked that.

KAREN (*as she thought*). No there isn't no vanilla in here.

LINDA. Is there not. Or it might have been peach then –

KAREN. Peach.

LINDA. – or maybe apricot –

KAREN. *Apricot?*

LINDA. – now I think of it yes. It was one of those sort of things anyway.

JONATHAN *crosses back in from outside.*

Maybe Jonathan'll know.

KAREN. Yes.

JONATHAN. Maybe Jonathan'll know what.

KAREN. I was just saying Jonathan. What kind of yogurt is it Edward likes?

JONATHAN. Yogurt?

KAREN. Yes.

JONATHAN. Uh –

LINDA. He says he doesn't want any breakfast but he might have some yogurt.

JONATHAN. – I mean God knows.

KAREN. I know he likes vanilla but there isn't no vanilla left.

JONATHAN. Okay.

LINDA. Is it peach he has sometimes, or is it apricot.

JONATHAN. I mean I have to say I wasn't aware that he was a big fan of either of those –

KAREN. No.

LINDA. No.

JONATHAN. – without wanting to be negative about it.

KAREN. It's funny they can get very particular at this stage.

LINDA. They can that. You're not kidding.

KAREN. I think I'll try the strawberry then –

JONATHAN. Yes.

LINDA. Yes –

KAREN. – give it a go.

LINDA. – yes no you can't go wrong with strawberry. I love strawberry, me.

KAREN *peels the plastic top off a yogurt.*

In the lobby, the door to The Room opens and SARAH *comes out.*

Hello Sarah.

SARAH. Oh hello.

LINDA. How are you today.

SARAH. Me? Yes no I'm fine thanks, yes.

GRAHAM. Ow fuck!

SARAH (GRAHAM, *the toaster*). What on earth's going on.

GRAHAM. What.

SARAH. I thought you were mowing.

GRAHAM. I was.

SARAH. Can't you take that outside.

GRAHAM. I'm doing it here.

SARAH. Honestly.

GRAHAM. I was saying to Jonathan, all it is it's the release mechanism. It's virtually solid. No wonder it's temperamental.

SARAH. *Temperamental?*

GRAHAM. When d'you reckon was the last time it was cleaned out.

SARAH. Oh God no –

JONATHAN. Yes –

SARAH. – no Mum used to do all that stuff.

GRAHAM. There you go then, four years. That'll be four years since it was cleaned out at least.

SARAH. He'd have a fit if he knew you had the bottom off out here.

GRAHAM. Yeah –

SARAH. *If it works, don't fix it.*

GRAHAM. – yeah the trouble with that philosophy Sarah, in Edward's case, nothing works.

SARAH. Yes –

GRAHAM. So in actual fact, *everything* needs fixing –

SARAH. – yes I *know*.

GRAHAM. – that's the trouble with that philosophy.

KAREN. We were just discussing Sarah. What kind of yogurt is it Father likes?

SARAH. Oh he's not having any yogurt now.

KAREN. Oh isn't he?

SARAH. No. He doesn't want any.

LINDA. Help.

KAREN. What does he want then?

SARAH. Nothing. He doesn't want anything.

LINDA. Does he not.

KAREN (*the yogurt*). Oh dear cos I've opened this now.

SARAH. Well never mind, someone'll have it later.

LINDA. Yes someone'll have it yes.

SARAH. What flavour is it?

KAREN. Strawberry.

SARAH. Right no he doesn't like strawberry anyway.

KAREN. Doesn't he?

SARAH. No.

KAREN. I thought he did. What flavour is it he likes then?

SARAH. I don't think he really likes yogurt very much.

LINDA. What not at all?

SARAH. Not really no.

KAREN. Oh.

LINDA. My husband was the same. That and beetroot. He wouldn't have it.

KAREN. He said he might have some.

SARAH. I know. Sometimes I think he says that just to shut people up.

KAREN. Yes.

SARAH. Sorry, I don't mean to –

KAREN. No that's alright dear. Funny really isn't it. A few weeks ago he was eating so well –

SARAH. Yes.

KAREN. – he had such a good appetite he did.

SARAH. Oh he's always had a good appetite. All his life.

KAREN. You will find this though.

LINDA. Yes.

KAREN. I mean this is the pattern, isn't it.

LINDA. Oh it is yes.

SARAH. Well. Anyway.

KAREN. Yes.

LINDA. Yes whereas me, I *love* yogurt.

SARAH. Right.

KAREN. Really.

Beat.

LINDA. Oh yes I love it. I don't know why.

SARAH. Well do *you* want it then?

LINDA. Me?

KAREN. You might as well, now it's open.

SARAH. Yes.

LINDA. Oh well –

SARAH. No go on, someone's got to.

LINDA. – are you sure?

SARAH. Yes of course, have it.

KAREN (*offering it.*) Here.

   Beat.

LINDA (*remind me*). What flavour is it again?

KAREN. It –

JONATHAN (*for fuck's sake*). It's *FUCKING STRAWBERRY.*

   They all turn to look at him.

   (*Normally.*) Sorry. I'm sorry. It's strawberry I think, isn't it.

KAREN. Yes.

LINDA. Well if you're sure.

   LINDA *takes the yogurt and crosses to find a teaspoon in a drawer.*

KAREN. Well how we shall persuade Edward to take his Oramorph now I don't know.

SARAH. Well he'll just have to take it won't he. It's not up to him any more.

KAREN. Maybe *you* can talk to him Jonathan.

JONATHAN. Well –

LINDA. Yes.

KAREN. He listens to his son doesn't he.

LINDA. Oh he does yes.

JONATHAN. – I mean I'll have a go.

KAREN. And maybe if Jonathan can't persuade him, maybe we'll have to wait for the nurse: is it –

SARAH. Julia.

KAREN. – Julia, yes.

LINDA. Yes Julia yes.

SARAH. Yes no he'll do whatever Julia wants him to do. I think we all know why.

LINDA. He's quite a character, your dad.

KAREN. He's a lovely man.

LINDA. He is a lovely man.

SARAH. Yes.

JONATHAN (*to* SARAH). What d'you mean *I think we all know why.*

SARAH. What?

JONATHAN. What does that mean?

A referee's whistle sounds from inside The Room.

LINDA. Oh right. Here we go.

SARAH. Yes –

LINDA. What now I wonder.

SARAH (*shaping to go in*). – I mean God knows. Could be anything.

LINDA. No you're alright love, I'll go in and see him –

SARAH. Well, really?

LINDA. – say good morning.

SARAH. Are you sure.

GRAHAM. What about your yogurt.

LINDA. That's alright love, it'll keep.

Beat.

GRAHAM. Right, okay.

LINDA. Why.

SARAH (*already on to it*). Okay no.

GRAHAM. What?

LINDA (*to* GRAHAM). Go on, what you thinking.

GRAHAM. Nothing.

LINDA. I've not touched it if –

GRAHAM. Right.

SARAH (*to* GRAHAM, *a command*). No.

LINDA. It's strawberry.

GRAHAM. Yeah I know it is.

LINDA. D'you like strawberry?

GRAHAM. I mean I do actually yeah –

LINDA (*why don't you have it then*). Oh well –

SARAH (*as above only more so*). *No* Linda.

GRAHAM. – since you mention it.

SARAH (*to* LINDA). It's *yours*.

LINDA. – no you're alright love, you're alright. (*Proffering it to* GRAHAM.) Here.

SARAH. That's *Linda's*.

GRAHAM. Yeah –

LINDA (*it's fine*). No no –

GRAHAM. – yeah I mean *is* it though?

LINDA (*good point*). Well –

SARAH. *Yes.*

LINDA. – I mean it's not *mine* is it.

SARAH. Yes it is.

JONATHAN (*half to himself*). Christ.

LINDA. I mean it's *Edward's* really isn't it.

GRAHAM. Yeah –

SARAH. Yes exactly yes, it's Dad's.

JONATHAN (*enough*). Look Sarah –

GRAHAM. – yeah but he doesn't want it does he.

KAREN. No

LINDA. No he doesn't no.

KAREN. No

GRAHAM. No. So –

JONATHAN. I mean for God's sake, can *somebody* just – [eat it.]

SARAH. He can't just appropriate anything Dad doesn't want.

GRAHAM. What?

SARAH (*completing her thought*). It's not right.

JONATHAN. – I mean *I'll* eat if for God's sake if that'll get rid of the fucking thing.

Another blast on the whistle, this time longer and more insistent.

KAREN. I'll tell you one thing. He's certainly got the hang of that whistle hasn't he.

LINDA (*crossing towards The Room*). He has that.

KAREN. Yes.

LINDA. Yes no he's a natural. (*Putting the yogurt down on the counter.*) What I'll do, I'll leave it here and you can all have a bit of a think shall I.

SARAH. Yes. Thank you Linda.

LINDA (*turning and heading towards the lobby*). Right.

GRAHAM (*fuck*). Right. Okay. Great.

JONATHAN. Yes great.

Another blast on the whistle.

LINDA (*shouting ahead*). It's alright Edward, here we come –

(*Pushing the door open.*) Good morning Edward. How are you today?

(*Sweeping cheerfully into the room.*) Now, what can I do for you. Is it a free kick or a penalty?

The door swings closed behind her.

Beat.

GRAHAM (*the kettle has boiled*). Okay, well. Who wants a cup of tea then.

JONATHAN. Yes –

GRAHAM. Karen?

KAREN. Oh yes please Graham.

JONATHAN. – yes great.

SARAH. No thanks.

KAREN. Are you sure Sarah.

JONATHAN. Yes –

SARAH. Yes.

JONATHAN. – you didn't have any breakfast did you?

SARAH. It's fine I'll have something later.

KAREN. If I was you'd I'd go home, have a nice shower, have a bit of a rest.

GRAHAM. Yes.

KAREN. We're here now we'll be fine.

Beat.

You've got to look after yourselves you know.

SARAH. Yes.

KAREN. All of you – for your sake and for Edward's.

SARAH. Yes I know.

KAREN. I know people keep telling you, but it's true. It takes more out of you than you realise.

SARAH. Yes.

KAREN. And really, it isn't like it's going to get any easier.

SARAH. No.

JONATHAN. No.

GRAHAM. No.

Scene Four, Late Morning

The sound of a lawn mower in some distant part of the garden. The church clock in the distance striking twelve.

Outside the back door, JONATHAN *on the phone pacing back and forth to try to find a good signal.*

As he talks, a MILKMAN *arrives along the path in the sunshine carrying a cradle of milk bottles.*

JONATHAN. Em can you hear me I just – Em? I lost you there for a moment…

Stopping pacing.

That's better… No okay that's better.

(*Resuming the conversation.*) No but we *have* talked about it, we *did* talk, in principle I mean… Well when you went up for it originally, otherwise… No but yes no of course, of course I am. It's just –

Signal break-up.

Em? Can you hear me?

(*Resuming.*) No it's just at the moment, I mean there's quite a lot going on here and it's like, you know? It's like – Em? Em? No you're… *Fucking signal*… Em can you hear me? I can't hear what you're saying you're – *Fuck.* Okay no Em I'm going to text you okay. I'm going to text you the landline number just in case you know if…

Signal finally gone.

Right, great. *Fuck!*

(*Becoming aware of the* MILKMAN.) Oh.

MILKMAN. Morning.

JONATHAN. Hi.

MILKMAN. Another lovely one.

JONATHAN. Isn't it, yes. Amazing.

MILKMAN. I didn't know many you wanted for the weekend.

JONATHAN. Yes. When is it you come again, Monday is it?

MILKMAN. Yeah Monday, yes.

JONATHAN. Right.

Beat.

I mean how many have you got with you there?

MILKMAN. I got six here with me now.

JONATHAN. Okay we'll have six then.

MILKMAN. I got more up on the van.

JONATHAN. No that's be fine. Six is a good number.

MILKMAN (*putting the bottles into the cradle*). How is Edward?

JONATHAN. Oh well he's, you know he's pretty ill now.

MILKMAN. Yeah.

JONATHAN. Yes.

MILKMAN. But hanging on I reckon –

JONATHAN. What? Yes no he's, you know –

MILKMAN. – yeah hanging on.

JONATHAN. Yes. So.

MILKMAN. I remember you you know.

JONATHAN. Who me?

MILKMAN. Yeah –

JONATHAN. Do you? How'd you mean?

MILKMAN. – walking up to catch the school bus in the mornings.

JONATHAN. Christ.

MILKMAN. Yeah you and your sister yeah. You used to say
good morning.

JONATHAN. God, yes –

MILKMAN. Very polite you were.

JONATHAN. – that was *you*.

MILKMAN. Yeah you wouldn't recognise me now. I was a young
man then.

JONATHAN. Yes, well me too –

MILKMAN. Yep.

JONATHAN. – me too.

MILKMAN. And you're up in London now though –

JONATHAN. Yes.

MILKMAN. – with the producing and that.

JONATHAN. Well yes. Yes.

MILKMAN. Yeah. Still. We must get on I suppose.

JONATHAN. Yes, true.

MILKMAN (*turning to go*). See you Monday then.

JONATHAN. See you Monday yes. Thanks. Really nice to meet you.

MILKMAN (*on his way back up the path*). Yeah very polite little boy and girl.

JONATHAN. Hh. Bye.

JONATHAN watches as the MILKMAN goes up the path with the empties and off.

Pause. He stands, thinking.

Then he goes back to his phone and becomes absorbed in composing a text.

Unseen by him as he thumbs at his phone, someone has arrived along the path from the gate and stopped at a distance taking in the house, the garden, the old trees, him.

A woman in her forties. NELL. She watches JONATHAN as he texts.

Eventually he finishes writing, hits send, and looks up.

Pause.

Hi.

NELL. Hello.

JONATHAN. You came then.

NELL. Yes. I wanted to see Edward.

JONATHAN. Yes, good.

Scene Four, Five Minutes Later

JONATHAN *flicks the kettle on then crosses to put the milk in the fridge.* NELL *stands taking in the room. A place she has known well.*

Outside the sound of mowing.

JONATHAN. What a fabulous morning.

NELL. Yes.

JONATHAN. It's amazing really, it's been like this for weeks. I mean it can't last.

Beat.

Tea? Coffee?

NELL. I'm fine thanks.

JONATHAN. Really?

NELL. Yes.

JONATHAN. I'm making one for myself.

NELL. No I'm good. Thanks.

Beat.

JONATHAN. So how *are* you.

NELL. Yes I'm okay, yes.

JONATHAN. You look well.

NELL. Yes. Yes.

A pause between them. Outside, the sound of mowing stops.

JONATHAN *busies himself with assembling things for his (instant) coffee.*

JONATHAN. Dad's actually through in the back room.

NELL. Right.

JONATHAN. I mean that's where he *is* now, you know we've, there's a special bed in there and – well you'll see.

NELL. Yes. How is he.

JONATHAN. Uhh well. I mean it's hard to believe really. It's incredible.

NELL. Yes.

Beat.

JONATHAN. How long did it take you to get down.

NELL. I suppose it took about five hours in the end.

JONATHAN. Right.

NELL. Yes.

JONATHAN. Well.

NELL. I set off early cos I need to get back.

JONATHAN. Yes.

In the lobby, the door to The Room opens and LINDA *comes bustling out.*

LINDA (*to* JONATHAN, *crossing to the kitchen*). Hiya.

JONATHAN. Oh hi Linda

LINDA (*to* NELL). Hiya.

NELL. Hello.

JONATHAN. Yes so Nell this is Linda.

LINDA. Hiya.

NELL. Hi.

JONATHAN. Linda's basically, she's –

LINDA. CareWatch Team Supervisor.

JONATHAN. – right yes, but she's basically a kind of Mother Teresa.

LINDA. I don't know about that Jonathan. I see the kettle's on.

JONATHAN. Yes. And this is Nell.

LINDA. Right.

NELL. Yes, hi.

JONATHAN. Nell's, she's just arrived –

NELL. Yes.

JONATHAN. – she's an old friend.

LINDA. Right so you're not an actress then.

NELL. What?

LINDA (*foot in mouth*). Ooh no –

NELL. Uh –

LINDA. Help –

NELL. – no I'm afraid not no.

JONATHAN. No.

LINDA. – honestly what am I like.

(*Busy with cups, etc.*) I'd do well to shut up sometimes, me. My husband used to say if my mouth was any bigger it wouldn't fit on the front of my face.

NELL. Right.

LINDA. And let's be honest, it's not a small face is it.

NELL. Anyway no, I'm not an actress.

LINDA. No.

JONATHAN. It was Nell that did that painting of the house. (*On the wall.*)

LINDA. No.

NELL. Well yes –

LINDA. You're kidding me.

NELL. – that was quite a long time ago.

LINDA. It's brilliant that is. You're a painter.

NELL. Well I'm actually a designer really.

LINDA (*no idea*). Oh right a designer yes.

NELL. Yes and I do a bit of teaching, so –

LINDA. Right.

NELL. – yes.

LINDA. No it is, it looks like a proper painting does that.

NELL. Yes well, thank you.

LINDA. And you've come to see Edward have you.

NELL. Yes.

LINDA. Yes well good for you, love. Good for you. Can I make you a cup of tea?

NELL. Oh no thanks –

LINDA. Are you sure.

NELL. – I'm alright for the moment. Thanks.

JONATHAN. I'm just making myself a coffee Linda if –

LINDA. No you are not Jonathan.

JONATHAN. Well – what?

LINDA. I'm making *you* one.

JONATHAN. No no –

LINDA. I've come out here –

JONATHAN. Okay well –

LINDA. – I'm going to make myself useful aren't I.

JONATHAN. Right.

> LINDA *crosses to the kettle and gets busy.*

> *In the lobby, the door to The Room opens and* SARAH *comes out.*

SARAH. Nell!

NELL. Hello Sarah.

> *A beat, then they're in each other's arms, holding each other in a tight hug.*

SARAH. God –

NELL. Yes.

SARAH (*into* NELL*'s shoulder*). – it's good to see you. It's good to see you.

NELL (*into* SARAH*'s shoulder*). You too. You too.

> *They hold each other, leaving* JONATHAN *and* LINDA *unsure what to do.*

Meanwhile, GRAHAM *has arrived from the garden at the back door in his shorts and boots.*

Eventually SARAH *and* NELL *unclasp each other.*

GRAHAM. Nell!

SARAH (*didn't see him*). Uhh God –

GRAHAM. Hello.

NELL. Hello Graham.

SARAH. – where the hell did *you* come from?

NELL (*crossing to kiss* GRAHAM *on the cheek*). Good to see you.

GRAHAM. Yeah you too yeah. Christ it's hot out there.

NELL. Yes. So I see.

SARAH. You've stopped.

GRAHAM. Yes. I thought I might have a cup of tea or something if there's one going.

LINDA. Yes –

SARAH. A cup of tea?

LINDA. – the kettle's boiled, love, there's plenty here.

As they continue, LINDA *drops teabags into a teapot, fills it from the kettle, assembles mugs, etc.*

SARAH (*to* NELL). How *are* you?

NELL. Yes I'm fine.

SARAH. You look great.

NELL. Really?

SARAH. Of course you do you look just the same you look fabulous. (*To* JONATHAN.) Doesn't she?

JONATHAN. Yes I mean –

GRAHAM. Yes she does yes.

SARAH (*to* GRAHAM). No not you.

GRAHAM. What?

NELL (*to* SARAH). How are *you*?

SARAH. Oh well I'm you know I'm okay, yes.

NELL. Yes.

Beat.

GRAHAM. I see you've stayed with Golfs then Nell.

NELL. What? Oh, yes.

SARAH. *What??*

GRAHAM (*what's the matter*). What.

SARAH. *Golfs??*

GRAHAM. I saw her car at the gate.

SARAH. Honestly, pathetic.

GRAHAM. What. You can't go wrong with a Golf.

SARAH (*to* NELL). Ignore him anyway, he's only come in cos
    he was hoping you might be the nurse.

GRAHAM. What?

NELL. The nurse?

GRAHAM. Look don't start that again okay?

SARAH. Julia.

GRAHAM. I ran out of petrol –

SARAH. Yes I bet you did.

GRAHAM. – I thought I might just as well come in for a cup of
    tea. How the hell did *I* know who was here?

Beat.

LINDA. Right who else is for tea then.

SARAH. Oh yes please Linda –

LINDA. Right.

GRAHAM. Great.

SARAH. – I'm parched.

NELL. Well actually maybe I will then –

LINDA. Yes.

NELL. – if everyone else is.

LINDA. I'll tell you what I'll say one thing for you Goulds. You can certainly shift some tea.

SARAH. I told Dad you might be coming.

NELL. Did you.

JONATHAN. Yes, did you?

SARAH. Yes. He was really pleased.

NELL. Really? He said that?

SARAH. Well I mean he's not really saying much now.

NELL. Right.

SARAH. Is he.

JONATHAN. No.

SARAH. No but I mean you could tell, you know you could really tell.

NELL. Right.

SARAH. I mean d'you want to come in and say hello.

Beat.

NELL. Uh yes I mean –

JONATHAN. Well –

NELL. – yes.

JONATHAN. – I mean hang on a minute Sarah.

SARAH. What.

JONATHAN. She's driven all this way –

SARAH. Yes no sorry –

JONATHAN. – she's barely got out of the car.

SARAH. – of course yes sorry Nell, I didn't mean to –

NELL. No it's fine.

JONATHAN. *Really?*

NELL. I came here to see Edward. That's why I came.

SARAH. Okay.

JONATHAN. Okay, well.

SARAH. You sure.

NELL. Of course, yes.

> *Beat.*

JONATHAN (*let's do it*). Right. Well –

LINDA. Hang on love what about your tea?

NELL. Oh, well –

LINDA. And there's your coffee here Jonathan.

JONATHAN. Yes –

LINDA (*to* NELL). It won't take a moment it's brewing here.

NELL. I mean maybe I'll have it afterwards –

SARAH. Yes me too yes.

JONATHAN. Yes.

NELL. – thanks.

LINDA (*offering a tin*). What about a biscuit to keep you going in the meantime.

NELL. Oh no thanks.

LINDA. You sure? Just in case.

NELL. No thanks, really.

SARAH. I will Linda.

> (*Taking one.*) Great, thanks.

GRAHAM (*reaching for the tin*). Yeah me too.

SARAH. Hang on you're not even going *in* there.

GRAHAM. What. I can still have a biscuit can't I? –

SARAH. Typical.

GRAHAM. – Christ.

JONATHAN. Right.

JONATHAN, SARAH and NELL cross to the lobby and to the door of The Room.

(*At the door.*) Okay?

NELL. Yes fine yes.

JONATHAN. Okay. Right.

JONATHAN pushes the door open.

SARAH. Dad, look who we've got.

NELL (*going in*). Hello Edward.

SARAH. Look who's come.

They go in and the door closes behind them. Pause.

In the kitchen, LINDA picks up the yellow file and starts to study it. GRAHAM finishes eating his biscuit.

GRAHAM. God it's hot out there.

LINDA (*at the yellow file*). Yes.

GRAHAM. I'll crack on again then. Take my tea out with me.

LINDA. Right-o love yes okay.

Beat.

GRAHAM. The thing is I want to go in there with them, I do want to. But I can't.

ACT TWO

Scene One, Early Afternoon

The play's theme establishes and fades.

GRAHAM on his own in the kitchen, in the process of screwing the toaster back up with a screwdriver. The church clock strikes three.

Outside, a nurse, JULIA, arrives along the path carrying her bag and pauses as she finishes a text message on her phone. Having done it, she puts the phone in a pocket, sets herself, then continues to the back step and knocks briefly on the open door.

JULIA. Hello?

GRAHAM. Oh hi Julia.

JULIA (*going in*). Anyone home?

GRAHAM. What yeah no yeah just me I'm afraid –

JULIA. Hello Graham.

GRAHAM. – yeah the others are all in with Edward.

JULIA. Oh right.

GRAHAM. Yeah so it's just me.

JULIA. It's another lovely day out there.

GRAHAM. Yeah I know. Come on in. Can I make you a cup of tea –

JULIA. Oh no thanks Graham.

GRAHAM. – or some coffee or maybe some other kind of you know –

JULIA. No thanks, no that's kind of you Graham. It looks like you've got enough on your hands there as it is. (*The toaster.*)

GRAHAM. What? Yeah no what it is – everyone's complaining about how useless the toaster is all the time. No one's ever thought to clean it out.

JULIA. Right.

GRAHAM. All the crap in here over the years. It's no wonder.

JULIA (*impressed*). You've fixed it.

GRAHAM (*modestly*). Yeah well you know it's nothing really –

JULIA. You say that –

GRAHAM. – it's just the release mechanism that's all. It's pretty standard stuff.

JULIA. – you're obviously a pretty handy man to have around.

Beat.

GRAHAM. Yeah no the thing with toasters is they're designed to do one thing. If they're not doing that they haven't got much going for them.

JULIA. Maybe you should come round to my place some time.

Half a beat.

GRAHAM. Yeah –

JULIA. Before you know it you'd be up to your ears.

GRAHAM. – yeah no that's yeah no yeah. Yeah.

JULIA (*crossing to the yellow file*). So how are things going?

GRAHAM. Yeah just about there I think –

JULIA. Right.

GRAHAM. – just plug it back in now basically.

JULIA. Yes. And how's Edward.

GRAHAM. Right. Yeah I think he's pretty weak now.

JULIA. Yes.

GRAHAM. But you know, he's so strong.

JULIA. Yes.

GRAHAM (*plugging the toaster back in at the wall socket*). Okay here we go. Stand back.

JULIA. Exciting.

GRAHAM. We can have some toast if you want.

JULIA. Yes. Great.

GRAHAM flicks the switch on at the wall and pushes the empty toast tray down in the toaster.

There's a bang and a flash as the plug blows at the wall, and all the ceiling spotlights go out.

Wooo!

GRAHAM. Right okay.

JULIA. You okay Graham?

GRAHAM. What yeah I'm fine yeah.

JULIA. You want to be careful there.

GRAHAM. Yeah fucking thing –

JULIA. You sure you're –

GRAHAM. – fucking useless. It's actually dangerous, bloody thing.

In the lobby, the door to The Room opens and SARAH comes out at speed.

SARAH. What the hell – oh hi Julia.

JULIA. Hello there Sarah.

SARAH (*to* GRAHAM). What the *hell* is going on?

GRAHAM. It's fine it's fine –

SARAH. For God's *sake* –

GRAHAM. – it's just a fuse.

SARAH. Everything's, there's no power in there, Dad's bed's stopped working.

GRAHAM. It's that bloody toaster –

SARAH. Right –

GRAHAM. – it's like you know, just get a new one for Christ's sake.

SARAH. – okay get it out of here.

GRAHAM. It's just the fuse that's tripped that's all.

SARAH. I don't care. I *knew* this would happen.

GRAHAM (*unplugging the toaster gingerly*). Alright okay keep your hair on –

SARAH. I *told* you to take it outside.

GRAHAM. – I'll just flick everything back on out here. (*Indicating the lobby.*)

In the lobby, the door to The Room opens and JONATHAN comes out.

JONATHAN. Right – oh hi Julia –

JULIA. Hello Jonathan.

JONATHAN. – everything okay.

GRAHAM. Yeah no it's all fine Jonathan –

SARAH. He's blown the bloody toaster up now.

GRAHAM. – it's just a fuse that's tripped that's all.

JONATHAN. Oh right, okay.

GRAHAM. I was saying to Sarah Jonathan, it's all very well but the trouble with this is it's knackered –

JONATHAN. Yes –

GRAHAM. – that's the basic problem with this.

SARAH. Well it definitely is now yes.

GRAHAM. Exactly, yes.

JONATHAN. Yes.

GRAHAM goes into the lobby, opens an old fuse box cupboard high up on the wall and starts fiddling inside it.

Sorry about this Julia –

JULIA. No no –

JONATHAN. – I didn't realise you were here.

JULIA. – no that's okay I've only just arrived.

JONATHAN. Would you like a cup of tea –

JULIA. No thank you Jonathan.

SARAH. A cup of tea?

JONATHAN. – or a coffee or –

JULIA. No thank you.

SARAH (*to* JONATHAN). *How?*

JONATHAN (*beat, looking at the kettle*). Oh right yes.

SARAH. Honestly.

JULIA. No Graham actually offered me one already.

SARAH. Yes I bet he did.

JULIA. I was saying to Graham – how is Edward today?

JONATHAN. Uhhhh well –

SARAH. Yes.

JONATHAN. – I mean I don't know maybe we should be trying to get him to eat something.

SARAH. How?

JONATHAN. Well we can't just do nothing can we.

SARAH. I'll tell you one thing. He's not going to be having any toast any time soon –

JONATHAN. No.

SARAH. – that's for sure.

JULIA. He's still resisting is he.

JONATHAN. Yes.

SARAH. He's resisting everything.

JULIA. I'll have a little chat to him.

JONATHAN. Yes –

SARAH. A little chat.

JULIA Yes.

JONATHAN. – I mean he does seem to listen to you.

JULIA. To be honest Sarah sometimes it's actually easier for someone outside the immediate family.

SARAH. Oh right.

JONATHAN. Yes maybe.

SARAH. Right well that must be it then. Yes.

JONATHAN. Also, there's his breathing now.

SARAH. Yes.

JULIA. His breathing.

JONATHAN. Linda thinks it's started to sound different.

JULIA. Okay.

SARAH. It does.

JULIA. When you say different Jonathan.

JONATHAN. I mean it might be nothing.

SARAH. No it does. He's definitely starting to struggle.

JULIA. Okay well I'll pop in shall I –

JONATHAN. I mean I don't know I can't tell any more now.

JULIA (*crossing towards the hall*). – I'll pop in and we'll have a little chat.

JONATHAN. Suddenly we're all experts on breathing.

The ceiling spotlights come back on.

SARAH (*the lights*). Right okay.

GRAHAM (*upbeat*). There you go.

JONATHAN. Good well that's something anyway.

GRAHAM. I told you: it's fine it's just a fuse.

SARAH. It's not a fuse. It's *you*.

JONATHAN (*moving on*). I'll come back in with you Julia shall I.

JULIA. Just as you like Jonathan –

JONATHAN. Yes.

JULIA. – it's up to you.

JONATHAN. Okay I'll follow you in.

JULIA *crosses to the lobby and pushes the door of The Room open.*

JULIA (*as she goes in*). Hello Edward. How are you today? It's me, Julia. Hello…

The door swings shut behind her.

SARAH (*doing Julia*). *I'll just pop in and have a little chat to him.*

GRAHAM. I think Edward's got a bit of a soft spot for her.

SARAH (*as above*). *Sometimes Sarah it's actually easier for someone outside the immediate family.*

JONATHAN. I mean I guess she's only doing her job.

GRAHAM. Yeah exactly.

SARAH. Oh for God's sake don't you start as well.

JONATHAN. What.

SARAH. You're all as bad as each other.

JONATHAN. What are you on about.

SARAH. It's pathetic. You know they played tennis together.

JONATHAN (*of course*). Yes.

GRAHAM. Who did.

JONATHAN. Edward and Julia, at the club yes.

GRAHAM. What he played with Julia.

SARAH. Exactly yes, for years.

GRAHAM. Blimey.

JONATHAN. Yes. So?

SARAH. Oh come on.

JONATHAN. No, what?

SARAH. They were *partners* –

JONATHAN. Yes –

SARAH. – *they played together, as a couple.*

JONATHAN. – yes I mean that's how mixed doubles works –

SARAH. What?

JONATHAN. – isn't it? That's how it *works*.

SARAH. Literally half his age. Him with his knee and everything. Pathetic.

JONATHAN. They were pretty good together actually.

GRAHAM. Yeah I bet.

SARAH. Yes well you *would* say that, wouldn't you.

JONATHAN. What does that mean.

SARAH. All that time. And you wonder why Mum got ill in the end.

JONATHAN. *What?*

SARAH *and* JONATHAN *looking at each other.*

Scene Two, Late Afternoon

In the garden outside the back door, NELL *has been helping* SARAH *take the washing off the line and put it in a basket.*

But she's stopped. She's been trying her best to hold herself together, and SARAH *has her arm around her.*

The sound of a lawn mower from somewhere off in the garden.

SARAH. Nell?

NELL. I'm sorry.

SARAH. No. Don't be silly.

NELL. I can't believe it.

SARAH. No.

NELL. I can't believe it.

SARAH. I know.

NELL. Anyway look at us. This is the last thing you need.

(*To herself.*) Come on get a grip.

SARAH. D'you want to sit out here for a bit.

NELL. Well, but I mean what about the washing.

SARAH. Never mind about the washing. Forget the washing.

They sit together on an old wooden bench.

Pause. Birdsong. The mower in the distance.

NELL. All the way down I was steeling myself.

SARAH. I know. Every morning I wake up and there's just like this moment, where you think everything's alright. And then you think oh no, of course.

Pause.

NELL. What a day.

SARAH. Yes.

NELL. The garden looks amazing.

SARAH. Yes –

SARAH. – yes well it should do. Every time the nurse arrives Graham appears and mows something.

Beat.

He should be out here really.

NELL. Who.

SARAH. Dad. He should be out here with his wheelbarrow, under some shrub or other, with a cup of tea going cold.

NELL. After I parked the car, before I came in, I went over into the churchyard.

SARAH. Oh right yes.

NELL. The flowers on Gill's headstone –

SARAH. Yes –

NELL. – they're really beautiful.

SARAH. – yes well someone's got to. Dad never went over there, not once, even before, even when he could.

Pause.

NELL. What's going to happen to it all?

SARAH. What the garden?

NELL. I mean everything, you know –

SARAH. Right yes –

NELL. – what's going to *happen*?

SARAH. – yes no I don't know. It'll be sold I suppose.

NELL. *Sold?*

SARAH. That'll be the next thing.

NELL. You haven't thought about –

SARAH. Me?

NELL. – you and Graham I mean, you haven't –

SARAH. Me and *Graham*?

NELL. Yes.

SARAH. That is a joke right? You are joking.

NELL. Right.

SARAH. Anyway we couldn't afford to even if we wanted to. No it'll be sold I suppose. That'll be the next thing to look forward to.

Beat.

It's his fault anyway.

NELL. What is. Graham's?

SARAH. No Dad's.

NELL. *Edward's?*

SARAH. If he'd just agreed to write a few more *Brian the bloody Badger* books when they were asking him to –

NELL. Hm.

SARAH. – we wouldn't be in this situation. He could've done it in his sleep. But no. Instead of insisting on writing a series of books on the *Meaning of the Fucking Garden.* We wouldn't be in this mess in the first place.

NELL. – I mean that's a bit harsh isn't it.

SARAH. It nearly drove Mum mad.

NELL. And Jonathan hasn't said anything about –

SARAH. Jonathan?

NELL. Yes.

SARAH. *God* knows what *Jonathan's* doing.

NELL. Right.

SARAH. God knows what he's thinking. But that's his stuff.

Beat.

All this stuff about he can't believe he won't be able to come here any more. I mean honestly. Huge great flat in London.

NELL. Yes –

SARAH. If he wanted it that much.

NELL. – I suppose it's not *that* big a flat.

SARAH. It's a flat. In London.

NELL. Yes.

SARAH. He could sell it – if he wanted to. Run his life from here. Half the people *round* here now are television producers anyway. You can hardly move for them.

Beat.

Anyway that's his stuff, that's his lookout. That's up to him.

NELL. It breaks my heart to see them together. Jonathan and Edward.

SARAH. Yes.

Pause. They sit in the sunshine.

NELL. You still teaching at the –

SARAH. Yes, still there.

NELL. Right.

SARAH. I went part-time last year. Just as well as it turned out.

NELL. Yes.

SARAH. Funny how things work out.

NELL. Yes.

Beat.

SARAH. And what about you.

NELL. Me.

SARAH. Are you still in Brighton.

NELL. Yes, yes –

SARAH. – and commuting in?

NELL. – yes, well some days yes.

SARAH. Right.

NELL. Most of it's online now anyway, you know –

SARAH. Yes.

NELL. – I don't really think they care where I am.

Beat.

SARAH. And still with Simon, is it –

NELL. Yes Simon yes.

SARAH. – yes.

NELL. Yes I mean he's away quite a lot so –

SARAH. Oh right.

NELL. – yes you know, he's always somewhere.

SARAH. Right.

NELL. Yes.

Beat.

And in the meantime here we are back on this bench again.

SARAH. Yep.

Pause. Birdsong. They take in the garden.

I did mean it you know, what I said then. Just so you know.

NELL. Right.

SARAH. I was going to do it, just in case you're wondering.

NELL (*confirming*). You mean Graham?

SARAH. I knew exactly what I was going to say to him: you know turn round, walk away, not look back. But when it came to it, when the moment came – I just, I didn't. I don't know why. I didn't say it.

Beat.

And then somehow, I don't know, the moment passed.

NELL. Yes well. Like you say, funny how things work out.

Pause.

Inside, the door to The Room has opened and JULIA *has come out with a plastic shopping bag tied tightly at the top, followed by* JONATHAN.

She crosses briefly to the yellow file to write something down, then follows JONATHAN *out of the open back door and outside.*

JONATHAN. Right. So.

SARAH. Yes so what's the news then.

JONATHAN. Yes.

SARAH. How is he.

SARAH *and* NELL *find themselves standing up.*

JONATHAN. I mean Julia d'you want to –

JULIA. – yes, thank you Jonathan. So Edward is actually quite a lot weaker now Sarah –

SARAH. Yes.

JULIA. – since I last saw him.

JONATHAN. Yes.

JULIA. So I'm going to ask Dr Parker to come and have a look at him.

JONATHAN. Yes.

SARAH. Dr Parker.

JULIA. This isn't to alarm you –

JONATHAN. No of course.

SARAH. No.

JULIA. But just to say, his pulse is weaker now –

SARAH. Is it.

JONATHAN. Yes.

JULIA. – he's running a bit of a temperature –

SARAH. Right. And what about the breathing.

JULIA. Yes. So Edward does seem to be starting to struggle now, you can hear it.

JONATHAN. Yes, I can hear it now.

JULIA. Yes. So it could be the start of an infection –

SARAH. Right.

JULIA. – maybe a chest infection or –

JONATHAN. Yes.

SARAH. Well his immune system's so clapped out.

JONATHAN. Yes.

JULIA. Yes it is, exactly Sarah that's right yes.

JONATHAN. So what happens now then.

SARAH. Yes.

JULIA. Well –

JONATHAN. More antibiotics.

JULIA. – well we could think about that Jonathan yes.

JONATHAN. Right.

JULIA. Although the metronidazole Edward's on at the moment is actually quite powerful already.

JONATHAN. Yes.

SARAH. So when you say we could *think* about it.

JULIA. I suppose what I'd say Sarah is, ultimately, antibiotics aren't going to cure this.

JONATHAN. Right, yes.

SARAH. No.

Pause.

JULIA. I mean you know, maybe have a think about it anyway.

JONATHAN. Right, yes. Maybe that's something we can ask Dr Parker when he comes.

JULIA. Yes, perhaps. In the meantime as I say I'll talk to Dr Parker and put him in the picture.

JONATHAN. Right.

SARAH. Okay.

JULIA. Okay, well –

JONATHAN. Thanks.

SARAH. Yes, thanks.

JULIA (*the tightly tied plastic shopping bag*). So I don't know what you –

JONATHAN. Yes uh –

SARAH. No give it to me that's fine –

JULIA. Really.

SARAH (*taking the bag*). – yes no I'll chuck it give it here.

JULIA. Okay well I'll be in touch then, and we'll take it from there.

JONATHAN. Right yes.

SARAH. Yes.

JULIA. Okay bye then.

SARAH. Bye.

JONATHAN. Yes bye Julia. Thanks.

JULIA. Bye.

NELL. Bye.

JULIA *goes up the path and leaves.*

JONATHAN. Right. Well.

SARAH. Great.

SARAH *crosses to the wheelie bin, opens the lid, and drops the orange bag in.*

Pause. Birdsong.

I think I'll go back in and sit with Dad for a while.

JONATHAN. Yes. Okay.

SARAH. If that's okay.

NELL. Yes.

JONATHAN. Yes.

SARAH *goes back into the kitchen, crosses through the lobby to the door of The Room and goes in.*

Pause.

Can I make you a cup of tea or something.

NELL. No. Thanks. I should be going really.

JONATHAN. Really?

NELL. Yes, I should get back.

JONATHAN. I mean up to you obviously. But it's a long way to come.

(*Glancing at his watch.*) I don't know what we'll be doing about eating, God knows. But I'm sure we'll be eating something, at some point. We'll have to.

Beat.

NELL. How d'you think this is for me.

JONATHAN. For *you?*

NELL. Coming back in through that gate again. Coming down the path.

JONATHAN. Yes well. I'm sorry it's not more fun. Believe it or not it's not exactly a barrel of laughs for me either.

NELL. I should never have come. I nearly didn't. But I wanted to see Edward.

JONATHAN. Yes good, so you said. Well now you have.

Pause.

NELL. I'm sorry –

JONATHAN. No –

NELL. – I didn't come down here to argue.

JONATHAN. – no I know. I know that.

NELL. I remember Edward saying to me once, we were sitting on the lawn out at the front having a cup of tea –

JONATHAN. Surely not.

NELL. – he was talking about the philosophy of the garden.

JONATHAN. Ah right yes. That.

NELL. He said what he wanted people to feel, he wanted to create a place, when you come in through the gate and it clicks closed behind you, you should feel that things are basically alright.

JONATHAN (*nothing*).

NELL. Whatever else is going on in your life, whatever problems, underneath everything else, deep down things are basically alright.

Pause.

JONATHAN *is nodding quietly to himself, trying to hold himself together.*

I should go.

JONATHAN *quietly shaking his head.*

I'm sorry. I'm sorry.

Scene Three, Evening

The play's theme establishes and fades.

Inside in the kitchen a bottle of wine (open) is on the table, which has been roughly laid for some kind of meal. Also a large bowl of Kettle Chips.

SARAH is sitting at the table nominally flicking through a newspaper, glass of wine in hand, munching Kettle Chips. NELL is at a window looking out at the garden in the evening light.

SARAH (*Kettle Chips*). Some more of these?

NELL. Uh, no thanks.

SARAH. Really?

NELL. Yes, I've probably had enough.

SARAH (*taking another handful*). Yes so have I.

> *Beat. SARAH munches.*
>
> (*Checking her watch.*) It's ridiculous. Where can he have got to?

NELL. Maybe he's hit traffic.

SARAH. Traffic?

NELL. Yes.

SARAH. Where?

NELL. Well or –

SARAH. He'd virtually have to go via Bristol to hit traffic.

NELL. Yes.

> *Beat. SARAH carefully selects one more single Kettle Chip and continues munching.*
>
> *Outside, GRAHAM appears purposefully along the path carrying five tightly bulging white plastic Chinese takeaway bags.*
>
> *He goes straight in to the kitchen and crosses to the table to put the bags down on the table.*

GRAHAM. Right, okay –

SARAH. Thank God.

GRAHAM. – here we are.

SARAH. Where the hell have you been?

GRAHAM. It's not my fault. They were busy. I drove like the clappers.

SARAH. You said you'd be half an hour.

GRAHAM. I would have been, but this great fat guy in front of me put in this enormous order.

SARAH. We've been getting light-headed.

GRAHAM. No wonder he was so fat.

GRAHAM *begins unpacking the plastic bags, taking out the tightly packed silver tinfoil cartons one after another.*

SARAH. You got everything.

GRAHAM. Yes.

SARAH. I'm starving.

GRAHAM. I got extra rice just in case.

NELL. Great.

SARAH (*trying to decipher the various scrawls on the carton lids*). Did you remember the kung pao prawns?

GRAHAM. Yes.

SARAH. And the noodles.

GRAHAM. Yes.

SARAH. And the pak choi?

GRAHAM. Yes. The what?

SARAH. The pak choi, in garlic sauce. For Nell.

Beat.

GRAHAM. Yep.

SARAH (*not seeing it*). You sure.

GRAHAM. It'll be in there somewhere. It's all here somewhere.

NELL. It smells good –

GRAHAM. Yeah –

NELL. – it smells great.

GRAHAM. – yeah it's not a bad place actually. It's often described as the best Chinese in the area.

SARAH. It's the only Chinese in the area.

GRAHAM. Yeah –

SARAH. It's rubbish.

NELL. I'll get the plates shall I. (*Crossing to the cupboard.*)

SARAH. Yes great.

(*To* GRAHAM.) Did you get some more soy sauce?

GRAHAM. No.

SARAH. No?

GRAHAM. I forgot.

SARAH. You *forgot*?

GRAHAM. Yes I forgot, okay? I went in there, I had a lot on my mind, they had some bottles of it like on the counter, I thought I must remember to get some of that, and I forgot. Okay?

SARAH. Great.

GRAHAM. That's how it happened.

In the lobby, the door to The Room opens and JONATHAN *comes out.*

JONATHAN. God that smells good Graham.

GRAHAM. Yep.

JONATHAN. You could smell it from in there.

SARAH. Yes there's no soy sauce I'm afraid, but apparently you can't have everything.

GRAHAM *has started spreading out the foil cartons on the table like a pack of cards.*

(*To* JONATHAN.) How is he.

JONATHAN. Not good. He's really struggling.

SARAH. Right.

GRAHAM. Right what have we got here –

(*Lifting the corners of carton lids in succession and sniffing.*) Prawn crackers – seaweed stuff – little prawn toast thingies – seaweed – beef something –

JONATHAN. Beef in black bean sauce.

GRAHAM. Yep.

JONATHAN. That's me I think.

GRAHAM (*sniffing again*). Actually no hang on that might be fish.

JONATHAN. Right.

GRAHAM. More seaweed –

SARAH. *More?*

GRAHAM. Noodles –

SARAH. Who ordered all this bloody seaweed?

GRAHAM. – Duck – Not quite sure what that is – Or that – rice –

(*To* SARAH.) Here you go here's your prawns in whatsit.

SARAH. Thank you.

GRAHAM (*continuing*). Noodles – More rice – stir-fried pork slices with peking-style sour green mustard in oyster sauce, that's me.

Beat.

Okay good. Dig in I think we're pretty much there.

SARAH. What about Nell.

GRAHAM. What?

NELL. No really –

GRAHAM. Haven't you got yours Nell?

NELL. – it's okay I'm sure it's –

GRAHAM. What was yours again?

NELL. Uh well it was pak choi actually, but –

GRAHAM. Pardon?

SARAH. I knew it.

NELL. Pak choi in garlic sauce, but really it doesn't matter.

GRAHAM (*sorting through the mass of cartons*). Hang on pak choi, pak choi…

SARAH. Did you ask for it?

GRAHAM. Just a minute it'll be here somewhere. What's it look like?

SARAH. What's it *look* like?

GRAHAM. Yes.

NELL. Well I mean it's just like a green vegetable in some garlic sauce basically, but –

SARAH. Yes.

GRAHAM. Right.

NELL. – but really –

GRAHAM. There's some fish here –

NELL. Yes –

GRAHAM. – sweet and sour by the looks of it.

NELL. Well that's –

SARAH (*to* GRAHAM). Did you actually *ask* for it?

GRAHAM. I'm sure I did.

NELL. – honestly, it doesn't matter.

GRAHAM. You can have some of my pork if you want.

NELL. Well –

SARAH. *Pork?*

GRAHAM. It's delicious.

NELL. Yes but –

SARAH. She's *vegetarian*.

Beat.

GRAHAM. What?

NELL. Yes.

SARAH. *She doesn't eat meat.*

GRAHAM. There's loads of seaweed.

JONATHAN (*enough*). Okay –

GRAHAM. Loads of the stuff here, look.

JONATHAN. – look why don't we just put everything in the middle of the table –

GRAHAM. Yeah –

NELL. Yes.

JONATHAN. – then we can all just share.

GRAHAM. – yeah exactly yeah share.

JONATHAN. Nell eats fish, don't you –

NELL. Yes.

JONATHAN. – so really it's fine.

GRAHAM. – yeah everybody can just have whatever they want, perfect.

SARAH. Yes just as long as you don't want pak choi yes. In which case you can't have any at all.

GRAHAM (*hitting the table explosively with his fist*). For Christ's *SAKE*!

Beat.

NELL. Really I'm fine –

SARAH. Or soy sauce.

GRAHAM. What is the *matter* with you?

SARAH. *Me?*

GRAHAM. Why are you so *angry* all the time?

SARAH. I'm not angry.

GRAHAM. Yes you are.

SARAH. I'm not.

GRAHAM. All you ever do is criticise. That's all you ever do.
And the thing is it's really easy to do, you know? Cos I can't
really answer back, can I? Not with all this going on. So I just
have to stand here and take it, in front of everybody, like some
bloody big stupid schoolboy. And it's not fair. It's not *fair*.

Beat.

SARAH. Guess what. I'm *upset*.

GRAHAM. *I'm* upset okay?

SARAH. I know.

GRAHAM. *I'm* upset. I can't even go *in* there. But why are you
angry with me? Cos you know, I'm doing my best.

SARAH. Yes.

GRAHAM. I can't do any more than I am doing.

SARAH. No. I know.

GRAHAM. Apart from anything else, it must be bloody
exhausting.

SARAH. It is yes.

GRAHAM. Yes. Well then.

SARAH. Yes.

Long silence. Some half-hearted eating.

JONATHAN (*taking the lid off a carton*). By the way I think
I've found the pak choi if anyone's interested.

SARAH. What?

GRAHAM. You've *found* it?

JONATHAN (*confirming*). Yeah here it is.

GRAHAM (*sniffing – a miracle*). Fucking hell.

JONATHAN. Right let's eat.

SARAH. Yes.

JONATHAN. I don't know about anyone else but I'm starving.

Pause. They all sit and start eating.

Outside, DR PARKER *appears along the path with his case. He pauses and takes a breath before knocking at the open back door.*

DR PARKER. Hi.

JONATHAN. Hello, come in.

DR PARKER (*coming in*). Something smells good.

JONATHAN. Yes.

GRAHAM. Yeah have some.

DR PARKER. Ah no thanks –

SARAH. Yes.

GRAHAM. There's loads of it here.

DR PARKER. – it's tempting though. Sorry if this isn't a great time.

JONATHAN. No –

SARAH. No not at all.

JONATHAN. – no thanks for coming.

SARAH. Yes.

DR PARKER. I got a bit held up, it's been one of those days.

JONATHAN. Yes.

DR PARKER. So how's things?

JONATHAN. Uh, not good I don't think.

SARAH. No.

DR PARKER. It's his breathing is it.

JONATHAN. Yes.

DR PARKER Okay.

JONATHAN. We thought we started to notice something different last night.

DR PARKER. Yes Julia had a conversation with me earlier.

SARAH. Yes, right –

JONATHAN. Yes.

SARAH. – she said she might talk to you. It's like he's really struggling now –

DR PARKER. Yes.

SARAH. – which is, you know, it's really –

DR PARKER. Yes, sure. Well I'll have a quick look at him shall I.

SARAH. Yes.

JONATHAN. Linda's in there with him at the moment.

DR PARKER. Okay. Great.

JONATHAN. I'll come in with you shall I.

DR PARKER. Uh well I don't want to disturb your meal.

JONATHAN. No well –

DR PARKER. I mean up to you, but maybe you should eat.

NELL. Yes.

JONATHAN. Okay.

DR PARKER. You know no hurry, take your time. In the meantime I'll go in and say hi.

JONATHAN. Right, yes.

> DR PARKER *crosses through to the lobby and goes into The Room.*

Right. Okay. Well.

> *Pause. They resume eating tentatively.*

GRAHAM. I mean I suppose it might not be pneumonia.

SARAH. What?

GRAHAM. It could be something else.

SARAH. Like what.

GRAHAM. I don't know.

SARAH. What else could it be?

GRAHAM. I don't know I'm just saying.

SARAH. Ridiculous.

GRAHAM. It needs to be something quick though. I mean not drawn out.

SARAH. It's already drawn out.

JONATHAN. Yes.

GRAHAM. Edward's suffered enough, surely.

SARAH. We could be here for weeks more knowing him. It'd be just like him.

They eat.

Suddenly the phone (landline) starts ringing.

(*Jumping.*) Christ.

JONATHAN. Ah okay –

SARAH (*getting up and crossing towards the phone*). I didn't realise this thing still worked.

JONATHAN (*standing*). – no it's, Sarah –

SARAH (*at the phone first, picking up*). Hello?… Yes… *Jonno??*…

JONATHAN. Sarah –

SARAH.…No sorry there's no one here called Jonno I think you've –

JONATHAN. – I'll take it – (*Already heading for the door to the hall.*)

SARAH (*on phone*) Oh *Jonathan* yes –

JONATHAN. – I'll take it in the hall.

Crossing into the hall and off, closing the door behind him as he goes.

SARAH (*on phone*). – yes sorry no Jonathan's here, he's just skipping along to the other phone I think…

Beat.

…Okay here he is yes okay bye.

(*Hanging up.*) Right okay. Good.

SARAH *returns to the table, sits down, and resumes eating.*

(*To* NELL.) So anyway, that's the doctor.

GRAHAM. Yes.

NELL. Right.

SARAH. Dr Parker.

NELL. Yes.

SARAH. Yes exactly.

GRAHAM. What?

SARAH. Nothing.

GRAHAM. Cuh –

SARAH. Nothing you'd understand anyway.

GRAHAM. – just cos he's a doctor.

SARAH. Well just cos Julia's a nurse.

GRAHAM. Don't start *that* again.

SARAH. We're all allowed to have our fantasies.

GRAHAM. No we're bloody not. Apart from anything else he always looks so tired.

SARAH. Well he probably is tired. That's all part of the appeal.

GRAHAM. Really?

NELL. Yes I can see that.

SARAH. I'm sure he is tired –

GRAHAM. He just looks clapped out to me.

SARAH. – I think his marriage is in trouble for start.

NELL. Really.

GRAHAM. Is it?

SARAH. I thought she'd left him, but then I saw them together in Morrisons the other day so I don't know what's going on.

GRAHAM. Left him why.

SARAH. I don't know do I? How do I know, it's just what I've heard.

GRAHAM. It's always the same with doctors.

SARAH. What is?

GRAHAM. Don't get me wrong though –

SARAH. That's a ridiculous thing to say.

GRAHAM. – I'm not saying it's easy being a doctor.

NELL. No.

GRAHAM. I wouldn't do it if you paid me.

They eat.

The door for the hall reopens and JONATHAN *comes back in.*

He sits back down at the table and resumes eating without saying anything.

Pause.

SARAH (*eventually*). Everything okay?

JONATHAN. What?

SARAH. Phoning on the landline –

JONATHAN. Oh right, yes –

SARAH. – I just thought –

JONATHAN. – no it's just, the mobile signal's so crap.

SARAH. Right, yes.

Beat.

How is she.

JONATHAN. Yes she's fine.

SARAH. Right.

Beat.

Any more news about Los Angeles.

JONATHAN (*giving her a look*). What?

GRAHAM. Los Angeles?

SARAH. Emma's been offered a job there.

GRAHAM. Has she?

JONATHAN. Well I mean –

GRAHAM. Wow.

JONATHAN. – yes but –

GRAHAM. What you mean like *LA*?

JONATHAN. – well yes but –

GRAHAM. Wow.

JONATHAN. – I mean these things are always –

GRAHAM. What a film?

JONATHAN. – no it's a actually Netflix thing but –

GRAHAM. Wow.

JONATHAN. – but it's all very you know –

GRAHAM. So what, she might be off to Hollywood then.

SARAH. Yes.

GRAHAM. Wow. So what would happen.

JONATHAN. Well –

GRAHAM. So what you'd go over there as well.

JONATHAN. I mean –

GRAHAM. You could *both* go.

SARAH. Yes.

GRAHAM. Blimey, LA.

JONATHAN. – I mean these things, you never really know
    what's happening so you know, it's –

GRAHAM. If you can make it there, you can make it anywhere.

SARAH. *What?*

GRAHAM. What.

SARAH. That's *New York.*

GRAHAM. What? Yeah, no I'm just *saying*. Who knows what might happen?

Pause. They eat. NELL *doing her best not to catch anyone's eye.*

In the lobby, the door to The Room opens and DR PARKER *comes back out, wrangling his stethoscope back into his case as he goes.*

DR PARKER. Hi.

JONATHAN. Hi.

SARAH. That was quick.

DR PARKER. Yes –

SARAH. Yes so what's the news?

DR PARKER. – yes so he's quiet now. Linda's going to stay in there with him.

SARAH. Yes.

JONATHAN. Good.

DR PARKER. So I've had a listen to his chest and lungs, we managed to turn him and I had a good listen front and back.

SARAH. Right.

DR PARKER. It is pneumonia.

SARAH. It is. Right.

DR PARKER. Yeah I'm afraid so.

JONATHAN. Right.

DR PARKER. You probably suspected as much.

JONATHAN. I thought it was.

SARAH. I don't know what I thought.

DR PARKER. It's in both his lungs. You can probably hear that little gurgling sound.

JONATHAN. Yes.

DR PARKER. I've given him a pretty big oxycodone injection which ought to help calm him down.

JONATHAN. I mean this is what you said would happen.

DR PARKER. Well yeah it can be a pattern, yes.

SARAH. So I mean does that mean –

DR PARKER (*ahead of her*). Right –

SARAH. – I mean what does that mean.

DR PARKER – yes.

(*Confirming.*) You've got someone coming in tonight.

JONATHAN. Yes.

SARAH. Yes.

JONATHAN. Karen's coming back later.

DR PARKER Right yes.

SARAH. Yes Karen yes.

DR PARKER. Cos as I say it's got a good hold in both his lungs, and he's got quite a fever running now as well.

JONATHAN. Yes.

SARAH. Right.

DR PARKER. Sorry just to appear with news like this in the middle of –

SARAH. No –

JONATHAN. No no –

DR PARKER. But on balance I reckon it's usually better to know.

SARAH. Yes.

JONATHAN. – yes of course yes.

DR PARKER (*taking out his card and scribbling on the back of it*). I'm going to leave you my mobile.

JONATHAN. Right. Thank you.

SARAH. Yes, thanks.

JONATHAN. Can I just ask a very basic question.

DR PARKER. Of course.

JONATHAN. So if, I mean how does it, do you need to be there –

DR PARKER (*ahead of him*). Right yes –

JONATHAN. – you know if, do we call you or –

DR PARKER. – I mean to be honest, as I say call me at any time, but the truth is I don't really need to be here no.

JONATHAN. Right.

DR PARKER. I'm sure Karen is excellent.

JONATHAN. Yes she is yes.

SARAH. Yes I mean she's great.

DR PARKER. It's really a time for the family now.

JONATHAN. Yes.

DR PARKER. Edward's actually very lucky in that respect. A lot of people aren't.

JONATHAN. Yes.

SARAH. Yes.

JONATHAN. Right.

DR PARKER. Okay then.

JONATHAN. Yes.

DR PARKER. I'm sorry you're having to go through this. It's really tough.

SARAH. And the stuff you've given him –

DR PARKER. The oxycodone yes.

SARAH. – yes cos he shouldn't have to suffer. I don't care what he wants.

JONATHAN. No.

SARAH. He shouldn't have to suffer like this. And we shouldn't have to watch him suffer. It's not fair.

DR PARKER. Well like I say the oxycodone should pretty much calm him down.

JONATHAN. Yes.

SARAH. It'll stop him struggling.

DR PARKER. It should do yeah.

JONATHAN. Right.

SARAH. It *should* do.

DR PARKER. Hopefully yes. But as I say, you know, call me if you feel you need to.

SARAH. Yes.

JONATHAN. Right. Well.

　Beat.

DR PARKER. Okay well I'll see you tomorrow then.

SARAH. Right.

JONATHAN. Will you?

DR PARKER. I'll probably look in in any case.

SARAH. Okay will you, right.

JONATHAN. Thank you.

SARAH. Yes, thank you.

DR PARKER. Yeah. Okay bye then.

SARAH. Bye.

JONATHAN. Yes.

DR PARKER (*to table*). Bye.

NELL. Bye.

GRAHAM. Thank you.

　　DR PARKER goes out of the back door. Outside after a few steps along the path, he stops, head bowed.

　　JULIA steps quietly out into view from the path. Pause. They hold each other.

　　In the distance the church clock begins to strike as they go back up the path together and off.

　　Back inside.

JONATHAN. Right. Well.

SARAH. Yes.

JONATHAN. Here we go.

SARAH. Yes.

GRAHAM. Yes.

The church clock continues to strike its way to nine.

ACT THREE

Scene One, Night

The play's theme establishes and fades.

The faint remains of late-summer light in the sky but it's nearly dark and the stars are out.

Outside, NELL is standing on her own, taking in the still night.

Inside, JONATHAN comes out of The Room and crosses through the kitchen to the back door.

He stops on the step and watches NELL for a while before she becomes aware of him.

JONATHAN. Hi.

NELL. Oh. Hi.

> *JONATHAN crosses towards her.*

> How is he.

JONATHAN. I've just come out for a bit.

NELL. Yes.

JONATHAN. He's fighting. He's not giving up.

> *Pause.*

NELL. I was walking round the garden.

JONATHAN. Yes.

NELL. It's so still.

JONATHAN. Yes, I know.

> *Another pause between them.*

NELL. What will you do.

JONATHAN. What. When.

NELL. Sarah says you're going to be selling the rectory.

JONATHAN. *Selling* it?

NELL. Yes.

JONATHAN. Who is?

NELL. Well she –

JONATHAN. She said that.

NELL. – she said it'll be sold.

JONATHAN. We haven't even *talked* about it. We haven't talked about that.

　　Pause.

NELL. Do you think you might go to LA –

JONATHAN (*non-committal*). Huh –

NELL. – and do all that.

JONATHAN. Yes.

NELL. When this is all –

JONATHAN. – yes I mean I don't know.

NELL. Do you think she wants you to.

JONATHAN. Who Sarah?

NELL. Emma.

JONATHAN. Oh right, yes. No I mean I don't know.

NELL. You don't know?

JONATHAN. I mean she might do, yes. I mean I think she probably does. I don't know.

NELL. And what about you.

JONATHAN. Me.

NELL. Yes.

JONATHAN. Well I mean it's, you know with everything. We haven't really had time to talk.

NELL. No. I bet.

JONATHAN. What.

NELL. I bet you haven't.

JONATHAN. What does that mean.

NELL. Nothing. It doesn't matter.

JONATHAN. My dad's dying okay. It's not a great time to talk about stuff.

NELL. No.

Pause.

JONATHAN (*a decision*). Okay. Okay. So when you walked in on Emma and me –

NELL. No.

JONATHAN. No come on let's do this.

NELL. Jonathan –

JONATHAN. No I don't care –

NELL. – please don't –

JONATHAN. When you walked in on us that night –

NELL. I'm sorry I'm not going back there. I'm not.

JONATHAN. – nothing had happened. Okay? Nothing. It was a possibility at that stage that's all. Maybe not even that, who knows.

NELL. So what's your point.

JONATHAN. Because the thing is, I even wonder, if you *hadn't* walked in –

NELL (*d'oh*). Oh I see, yes –

JONATHAN. – if that hadn't happened.

NELL. – I get it.

JONATHAN. No I'm just –

NELL. It was *my* fault for walking in.

JONATHAN. That's not what I meant.

NELL. What did you mean then.

JONATHAN. Emma was going through – she was all over the place. She didn't know what she was doing.

NELL. How dare you?

JONATHAN. I'd never been in that situation before. And then suddenly everything –

NELL. How *dare* you do this? *Now?*

JONATHAN. Well you started this. If you want to talk.

NELL. It's incredible. It's as if you aren't *in* this. As if you weren't even *there*. But that's it of course isn't it.

JONATHAN. I'm sorry I don't really know what that means.

NELL. Do you love her?

JONATHAN (*enough*). Okay –

NELL. Are you going to have kids?

JONATHAN. Look –

NELL. Have you *had* any of those conversations?

JONATHAN. Okay shall we stop this now.

NELL. You don't know what's going to happen to all this; you don't know whether you're going to go out to LA; you don't know if you love her; you don't know if you'd even be with her if I hadn't walked in.

Beat.

It's like you're frightened. Like you aren't present in your own *life*.

JONATHAN. Frightened?

NELL. Frightened of love.

JONATHAN. That's ridiculous. And you know it is.

NELL. And really, I feel sorry for you, you know? Because really, it's the last thing you should be frightened of, love.

Pause.

JONATHAN. Well that's something, coming from you.

NELL. What?

JONATHAN. I mean that's really something.

NELL. What d'you mean by that.

JONATHAN. From someone who thought she was pregnant, I mean who *was* pregnant, but didn't actually tell her partner.

Pause.

NELL. What so you – [know?]

JONATHAN. She's my *sister*.

NELL. But I made her promise not to –

JONATHAN. Yes I'm sure you did yes. But you tell someone something like that, what *else* are they going to do.

Beat.

NELL. I was going to tell you –

JONATHAN. Were you.

NELL. – obviously.

JONATHAN. *Obviously?*

NELL. Well anyway in the end there was nothing to tell you was there. So.

Pause.

JONATHAN. Nothing to *tell* me.

NELL. Not as things turned out, no.

Beat.

JONATHAN. But you told Sarah though anyway, you phoned her.

NELL. Yes, but that's different.

JONATHAN. Is it?

NELL. Yes.

JONATHAN. How do you think I felt when –

NELL (*cutting him off*). I *wanted* to tell you okay.

JONATHAN (*so why didn't you*). Okay –

NELL. I wanted to tell you everything I felt.

JONATHAN (*as above*). Okay, so then –

NELL. More than *anything*. But by then, well, Emma. Basically.

JONATHAN. Emma.

NELL. By then you weren't my partner any more, were you.

Pause. They stand there looking at each other.

KAREN. Hi there.

JONATHAN. Oh hi Karen.

KAREN *has appeared along the path carrying her bag.*

KAREN. What an evening.

JONATHAN. I know, beautiful isn't it.

KAREN. It's perfect. I come in through Aveton Gifford and along by the river through the valley tonight.

JONATHAN. Oh yes.

KAREN. Lovely it was. I saw a badger.

JONATHAN. Oh really.

NELL. A badger?

KAREN. Yes.

JONATHAN. Where?

KAREN. A real one I mean. Trotting along the road at the top of the hill he was, minding his own business. I stopped the car and turned the headlights off, cos they get a bit confused in the headlights.

JONATHAN. Yes.

KAREN. He had a look at me, I had a look at him, and then he just continued on wherever he was going, through a gap in the hedge.

JONATHAN. And you continued on where you were going.

KAREN. Exactly yes. Exactly. It was comical really.

JONATHAN. Yes.

KAREN. How's Edward?

JONATHAN. Uh – not good really.

KAREN. No.

JONATHAN. Dr Parker came and had a look at him.

KAREN. Yes.

JONATHAN. He's got pneumonia now.

KAREN. Oh yes. Has he.

JONATHAN. It's in both lungs. Yes. So.

KAREN. And how are you?

JONATHAN. Me?

KAREN. Yes.

JONATHAN. I was in there, but I came out for a bit.

KAREN. Yes.

JONATHAN. Sarah's in with him at the moment, and Linda's still here.

KAREN. He's fighting it I suppose is he.

JONATHAN. Yes.

KAREN. Yeah, course he is, Edward. It's a good thing though really isn't it Jonathan.

JONATHAN. What is.

KAREN. Course they used to call it Old Man's Friend.

JONATHAN. Yes.

KAREN. Cos really, I know he wanted to come back to the house and the garden and that, he's where he wanted to be. But really I don't know how much he's really –

JONATHAN. No.

KAREN. – he's been so ill.

JONATHAN. Yes.

KAREN. So it is a good thing really. Yeah Old Man's Friend they used to call it, years ago. I'll go in and say hello.

JONATHAN. Right yes. I'll come back in with you.

KAREN. Well you just take your time Jonathan, it's lovely out here. It's such a nice night.

JONATHAN. Yes.

KAREN. There's nothing to be frightened of.

Beat.

JONATHAN. No.

KAREN. I always say that cos people worry how they'll be. There's nothing to be frightened of at all.

KAREN continues along the path to the back door and into the kitchen, leaving NELL and JONATHAN outside.

Scene Two, Night

In the kitchen.

GRAHAM *at the kettle handing out mugs of tea to* JONATHAN *and* NELL.

GRAHAM (*passing a mug of tea to* NELL). There you go Nell.

NELL. Thanks.

JONATHAN. Thanks Graham, great.

GRAHAM (*proffering a tin*). Biscuit anyone?

NELL. No thanks.

JONATHAN. No.

GRAHAM (*taking one himself*). Got to keep your strength up. I don't suppose we'll be getting much sleep tonight.

JONATHAN. Well no.

GRAHAM. Or maybe we will, who knows.

Pause. They sip tea. GRAHAM *munches his biscuit.*

God what a night out there.

JONATHAN. Yes.

GRAHAM. I was walking round the garden. Have you seen the stars?

NELL. Yes.

GRAHAM. I don't think I've ever seen them so bright.

In the lobby, the door to The Room opens and SARAH *comes out.*

JONATHAN. Hi.

SARAH. Hi.

GRAHAM. There's some tea there.

SARAH. I had to come out.

JONATHAN. Yes. I know.

GRAHAM (*passing a mug of tea to* SARAH). Here have this. That'll put hairs on your chest.

SARAH. *What?*

GRAHAM. There's some biscuits here too if you want.

GRAHAM offers her the tin. It's as if she hasn't heard him. He puts it back down again.

Outside, an owl hoots from a tree somewhere in the garden.

Huh. Everyone's out tonight.

JONATHAN. Yes.

GRAHAM. Karen saw a badger earlier.

JONATHAN. Yes.

GRAHAM. Funny.

SARAH. I still can't believe it.

NELL. No.

JONATHAN. No, I know

Beat.

GRAHAM. What, badgers?

SARAH. No *this*.

GRAHAM. Oh right yes.

SARAH. Any of it, even now.

GRAHAM. I was going to say. Cos you see 'em quite often down in the valley there actually.

Beat.

JONATHAN. You know what it reminds me of, a bit.

SARAH. What.

JONATHAN. Remember the eclipse.

SARAH. Yes. Of course.

NELL. Yes.

JONATHAN. That morning.

GRAHAM. Yeah I remember that. You and Nell came down.

NELL. Yes.

GRAHAM. We all walked up the village together and stood in the top field there, waiting.

SARAH. Yes. Mum and Dad didn't come. He wanted to be in the garden of course.

JONATHAN. Yes. Anyway. I knew exactly what was going to happen: I knew *why* it was going to happen, I knew when, but when it did –

NELL. Yes.

JONATHAN. – I couldn't believe it. It went quiet, the birds gradually stopped singing, everything very still –

NELL. Yes.

GRAHAM. Yeah it was weird.

JONATHAN. Then suddenly it came. The horizon out over the coast went black, and I thought oh my God here it comes, it's actually going to happen. My legs went underneath me. I just could not believe it.

SARAH. No.

JONATHAN. This is like that.

SARAH. Yes.

Pause.

The thing is though, with the eclipse, it came light again after a few minutes.

JONATHAN. Yes.

SARAH. Then it was a normal day again.

JONATHAN. Yes.

In the lobby, the door to The Room opens and LINDA *comes out.*

LINDA. Hiya.

GRAHAM. Hi Linda

LINDA *crosses to write something in the yellow file.*

LINDA. Right. Just fill in my stuff. Honestly you could make a book out of this. You could publish it.

NELL. Yes.

GRAHAM. I've just made some tea here if you want some.

LINDA. No thanks love.

GRAHAM. Or some coffee.

LINDA. No thanks I should be off. Karen's here now.

GRAHAM. Right.

LINDA *finishes her entry in the file.*

LINDA. Right. That's me done.

SARAH. What so you're off are you? You're going.

LINDA. I'm all done, love, yes.

GRAHAM. You sure you won't have a cup of tea before you go.

SARAH. Yes.

LINDA. No you're alright Graham –

GRAHAM. There's loads of it here.

LINDA. – I'd best keep going. Like I say Karen's here now –

JONATHAN. Yes.

LINDA. – and you know I've said cheerio and what-have-you.

SARAH. Yes. Right, well.

JONATHAN. And if anything does happen, obviously –

LINDA. Oh no they'll tell me, love.

JONATHAN. Oh okay –

LINDA. Yes.

JONATHAN. – I wasn't sure how it worked.

LINDA. No they tell me. That all happens automatically.

JONATHAN. Right, okay. Well look, thanks again then Linda.

SARAH. Yes, thanks.

LINDA. No it's a pleasure, love. You should be proud of yourselves, you know that.

SARAH (*modesty*). Well –

LINDA. Never mind *well* Sarah. I'm from Lancashire, and you've done brilliant. All of you.

JONATHAN. Well thanks anyway.

SARAH. Yes, thanks. Thanks.

LINDA. I'll not forget this. I'll tell you that for nothing.

SARAH. No well. Us neither I suppose.

LINDA. I'll not forget this place.

JONATHAN. No.

Beat.

LINDA. I'll see ya then.

SARAH. Goodnight.

JONATHAN. Yes.

LINDA (*to* NELL). Bye love.

NELL. Bye.

GRAHAM. Bye.

Beat. Then LINDA *turns, crosses to the back door, and goes off along the path without looking back.*

Pause.

She's nice, isn't she?

JONATHAN. Yes.

GRAHAM. Nice woman.

JONATHAN. Yes.

SARAH. Yes.

Scene Three, Night

In the kitchen, GRAHAM *on his own flat-out asleep in a chair with a newspaper open on his knees.*

NELL *is standing at a window looking out into the night.*

Silence.

Then NELL *turns and crosses to the sink to pour herself a glass of water as quietly as she can.*

GRAHAM (*jerking awake*). Uhhh Jesus.

(*Checking his watch.*) What time is it.

NELL (*a guess*) Half past four?

(*Her watch.*) Half four yes.

GRAHAM. Right.

(*The paper.*) The fourth bloody time I've read this article.

NELL. Really.

GRAHAM. Wasn't any good the first time: I can't help it if we're all getting fatter can I.

NELL. No

GRAHAM. Not all of us, obviously. I mean I am probably. I must be.

GRAHAM *hauls himself up out of the chair and crosses to the biscuit tin on the table.*

D'you want one of these?

NELL. No thanks Graham.

GRAHAM. No. *I* shouldn't either really, but these are not normal times. (*Taking a biscuit.*)

NELL. No.

GRAHAM (*munching*). It's hard to imagine things getting back to normal after this though. I don't suppose they do from now on, not really.

NELL. No.

GRAHAM. I know Sarah still misses her mum.

NELL. Yes.

GRAHAM. I mean I do too obviously.

NELL. Yes. Well me too.

GRAHAM. Yeah she really liked you, you know? But you know, Sarah could talk to Gill.

NELL. Yes.

GRAHAM. And then with Edward, same thing really. I don't know what we shall do now. I suppose we'll have to talk to each other.

NELL. Well maybe.

GRAHAM. God knows how that's going to work.

In the lobby, the door to The Room opens and JONATHAN *comes out.*

JONATHAN. Hi.

GRAHAM. Hi Jonathan. How's it going in there.

JONATHAN. It's pretty quiet now.

GRAHAM. Yes.

JONATHAN. He hasn't opened his eyes for the last couple of hours.

GRAHAM. No. Want one of these?

JONATHAN. No thanks.

GRAHAM. It'll be coming light soon.

JONATHAN. Yes.

GRAHAM. Then we're into another day. You never know, Edward might have his own ideas. Nothing would surprise me.

JONATHAN. No.

GRAHAM. At this rate we could run out of biscuits altogether.

JONATHAN. I don't know whether he knows we're there. I hope he does.

GRAHAM. They say the hearing's the last thing to go.

JONATHAN. Yes.

GRAHAM. I reckon he knows.

JONATHAN. I thought he squeezed my hand a while a go. But that might just have been me.

GRAHAM. I was saying to Nell, it's hard to think of things getting back to normal after this.

JONATHAN. Yes.

GRAHAM. Tell you one thing. It's funny to think of other people being at the rectory. You know, driving past the gate…

In the lobby, the door to The Room opens and KAREN *steps out.*

JONATHAN. Hi.

KAREN. Hi.

JONATHAN (*something in her demeanour*). Is everything –

KAREN. I think maybe you should come back in now maybe.

JONATHAN. Oh okay, right.

KAREN. He's going, yes.

JONATHAN. Right. Thanks.

KAREN. If you want to.

JONATHAN. Yes, yes thanks Karen thanks. Right.

KAREN *turns to go back.*

(*To* NELL.) Uh –

NELL. I'll stay out here shall I.

JONATHAN. – well but not if you –

NELL. No you go.

JONATHAN. You sure cos –

NELL. Yes you go, you go.

JONATHAN. Okay.

(*To* GRAHAM, *confirming.*) And you're staying here Graham.

GRAHAM (*let me think*). Uh –

JONATHAN. Up to you obviously.

GRAHAM (*beat, then casually*). No I think I'll come in actually.

JONATHAN. Right.

GRAHAM. Yeah might as well.

KAREN, JONATHAN *and* GRAHAM *cross to the lobby and off into The Room. The door closes behind them.*

NELL *is left standing in the kitchen on her own.*

Pause.

She crosses to the sink, finds a glass, pours herself a glass of water. Takes a sip. Stands there.

Silence. The house quiet.

Then she turns, crosses to the lobby and goes in.

Scene Four, Dawn

In the lobby, the door to The Room is open.

KAREN *is standing at the yellow file filling in a series of tick-box questions on a form. She gets to the end and reviews what she's done.*

NELL *comes slowly out of The Room.*

NELL. Amazing.

KAREN. Yes.

NELL. It's incredible.

KAREN. This your first time is it.

NELL. What? Yes –

KAREN. Yes.

NELL. – yes it is. *So* peaceful.

KAREN. Oh it is. He is peaceful now, after all he's been through.

NELL. Yes.

KAREN. He was a lovely man, Edward –

NELL. Yes.

KAREN. – lovely. You could just tell.

NELL (*crossing to the window*). Is it coming light.

KAREN. It might be.

NELL. It is, yes.

KAREN. Yes.

NELL. Strange really. Another day.

SARAH *comes slowly out of The Room, crosses to kitchen and stands.*

Beat.

SARAH. Well. That's that.

KAREN. Yes. It's over now Sarah –

SARAH. Yes.

KAREN. – it's over, no more suffering. We were just saying –
he looks so peaceful now.

NELL. Yes.

SARAH. That's it as far as parents go anyway. No more parents.

KAREN. Poor Edward, he suffered enough.

Beat.

SARAH. Where's Graham?

KAREN. He went outside I think.

SARAH. *Outside?*

KAREN. Yes.

SARAH. What *for*? (*Crossing to the back door.*)

KAREN. He went out into the garden.

SARAH *crosses outside.*

SARAH. Graham? Graham?

GRAHAM (*off*). It's alright –

SARAH. Where are you.

GRAHAM (*off*). – I'm just here.

SARAH. What are you *doing* out here?

GRAHAM *appears from the path to the garden.*

GRAHAM. I've been out in the garden.

SARAH. I didn't know where you were.

GRAHAM. It's coming light look.

Beat.

You okay? I've just been round the garden.

SARAH. I didn't know where you were.

Suddenly she hugs him. Holds him.

GRAHAM. It's over now.

SARAH *buries her head in his shoulder.*

It's over. I'm here.

They hold each other. He kisses the top of her head.

The first birdsong – a single blackbird starting to sing.

Come on.

They unclasp each other and walk slowly along the garden path hand in hand and off as –

– inside, JONATHAN *comes out of The Room. He pauses in the open door and turns to look back before crossing slowly into the kitchen.*

JONATHAN. It's coming light.

KAREN. Yes.

I'll go in and open the curtains in there shall I.

JONATHAN. Uh yes –

KAREN. Let the day in.

JONATHAN. – yes if you like, yes.

KAREN. I think Edward might like that somehow.

JONATHAN. Yes, he would yes. Good idea.

KAREN *crosses through to the lobby and goes off into The Room.*

Pause. NELL *and* JONATHAN.

I'm going to go and walk round the garden.

NELL. Yes, okay.

JONATHAN. I don't know why really, but –

NELL. Yes.

JONATHAN. – anyway.

NELL. Are you okay?

JONATHAN. Yes, I'm okay. Yes.

Beat.

Pause.

Another brief burst of birdsong.

D'you want to come with me. Shall we walk round the garden.

Beat. No response from NELL.

If you want to.

And another burst of birdsong.

Hh – blackbird.

NELL. Yes. Is that what it is?

JONATHAN. It's morning.

NELL. Yes.

JONATHAN. Yes.

NELL *and* JONATHAN *turn and stand looking at each other.*

Another blackbird starts to join the first one in full throat. Then another.

It gets lighter.

White-out.

End.